SHERWOOD ANDERSON / GERTRUDE STEIN
Correspondence and Personal Essays

Sherwood /Gertrude
Anderson /Stein

Correspondence and Personal Essays

Edited by RAY LEWIS WHITE

The University of North Carolina Press
Chapel Hill

Manufactured in the United States of America
Printed by Heritage Printers, Inc., Charlotte, North Carolina
ISBN 0–8078–1197–1
Library of Congress Catalog Card Number 72–78152

The University of North Carolina Press and the editor wish
to express their gratitude to the following for permission to
reprint copyrighted material:

To Eleanor Copenhaver Anderson for material from:
  The Flowers of Friendship: Letters Written to Gertrude
  Stein, ed. Donald Gallup (New York: Alfred A. Knopf,
  1953), pp. 142–43, 144–45, 152–53, 155–56, 179, 191–
  92, 211–12, 226–27, 353–54.
  "Four American Impressions," New Republic 32 (11 October 1922):171–73; reprinted in Sherwood Anderson's
  Notebook (New York: Liveright, 1926), pp. 47–55.
  Copyright 1922 by The Republic Publishing Company;
  copyright renewed 1949 by Eleanor Copenhaver Anderson.
  "Gertrude Stein," American Spectator 2 (April 1934):3;
  reprinted in No Swank (Philadelphia: Centaur Press,
  1934), pp. 81–85. Copyright 1934 by American Spectator, Inc.; copyright renewed 1961 by Eleanor Copen-
  haver Anderson.
  Letters of Sherwood Anderson, ed. Howard Mumford
  Jones and Walter B. Rideout (Boston: Little, Brown and
  Company, 1953), items 67, 69, 75, 76, 109, 240, 257,
  334. Copyright 1953 by Eleanor Copenhaver Anderson.
  A Story Teller's Story: A Critical Text, ed. Ray Lewis
  White (Cleveland: Press of Case Western Reserve University, 1968), pp. 260–61, 263, 271–72. Copyright 1924
  by B. W. Huebsch, Inc.; copyright renewed 1951 by
  Eleanor Copenhaver Anderson.

To Daniel C. Joseph, Administrator of the Gertrude Stein
estate and for the heirs of the late Gertrude Stein, for material
from:
  "Idem the Same—A Valentine to Sherwood Anderson,"
  Little Review 9 (Spring 1923):5–9.
  Introduction to Gertrude Stein's Geography and Plays
  (Boston: Four Seas Company, 1922).
  Review of Sherwood Anderson's Puzzled America, in Chi-
  cago Daily Tribune, 4 May 1935, p. 14.
  Review of Sherwood Anderson's A Story Teller's Story, in
  Ex Libris 2 (March 1925):177.
  "Sherwood's Sweetness," Story 19 (September–October
  1941):63.

To Random House, Inc., for material from:
  The Autobiography of Alice B. Toklas (New York: Har-
  court, Brace and Company, Inc., 1933), pp. 241–42, 265–
  66, 302–4. Copyright by Random House, Inc.
  Everybody's Autobiography (New York: Random House,
  Inc., 1937), pp. 222–23, 256, 257, 270, 271–72.

In honor of
MARK SCHORER

ACKNOWLEDGMENTS

I am pleased to acknowledge the help and the encouragement of the following people in my preparation of this book: Henry H. Adams, Illinois State University; Eleanor Copenhaver Anderson, Marion, Virginia; Carlos Baker, Princeton University; Earle E. Coleman, Princeton University Library; Lambert Davis, director emeritus, The University of North Carolina Press; Michael Fanning, Southeastern Louisiana College; Donald Gallup, Beinecke Rare Book and Manuscript Library, Yale University; Milton Greenberg, Illinois State University; Diane Haskell, manuscripts curator, The Newberry Library; Arlan Helgeson, Illinois State University; C. Hugh Holman, The University of North Carolina at Chapel Hill; Adam D. Horvath, Press of Case Western Reserve University.

Also Richard Johnson, bibliographer of American literature, The Newberry Library; Calman A. Levin, Baltimore, Maryland; Patricia Powell, Harold Ober Associates; William Simms, Chicago, Illinois; Lawrence W. Towner, director, The Newberry Library; James M. Wells, associate director, The Newberry Library; Ivan von Auw, Harold Ober Associates; and Gary Lee Zeller, Emerson College.

Illinois State University   R.L.W.

SHERWOOD ANDERSON / GERTRUDE STEIN
Correspondence and Personal Essays

No one has ever been quite sure just what to make of the friendship of Sherwood Anderson and Gertrude Stein. Anderson always claimed that Gertrude Stein's writing influenced his own literary style. Miss Stein always claimed to have great affection and appreciation for Sherwood Anderson. Both authors claimed to have influenced the course of American writing—through their own publications and through having taught the basics of fiction to such younger writers as Ernest Hemingway. There are few enough facts available to document these claims of friendship and influence. After all, what sort of friendship could be expected between a sophisticated, highly educated esthete like Gertrude Stein and a comparatively uneducated, naïve, midwestern ex-businessman like Sherwood Anderson?

Whatever the basis of this friendship, it has become part of the folklore of American literary history that the relationship was indeed important. Attempts to demonstrate its importance have resulted only in commonplaces about "influence" and "mutual appreciation." But there exists a large body of correspondence between Sherwood Anderson and Gertrude Stein, as well as several personal essays the two wrote about each other. At this remove, one is unlikely to learn more about the depth and breadth of the literary friendship than from these documents. Publication of this material might reveal the relationship to have been sincere if fairly superficial, or perhaps the documents will finally confirm that the Anderson-Stein bond deserves its status as legend—as the lives of the authors are legendary in American literature.

Sherwood Anderson made of his own youth and early manhood the legend of his life; Gertrude Stein became legendary only after escaping from all aspects of her early years. There could scarcely be more contrast in childhood experience than between Sherwood Anderson and Gertrude Stein. Anderson was born in the village of Camden, Ohio, on September 13,

1876. The third child in a large family, he enjoyed the most ordinary of parents—a relatively uneducated, profligate father who made horse harness and a dull, hard-working mother who assumed control of her family by support instead of through love. So ordinary was Anderson's youth in the town of Clyde, Ohio, where his family moved in 1884, that he afterward romanticized his family into a heroically sad father who told tall tales and drank instead of working; a pathetically long-suffering mother who washed other people's clothes and defied her impoverished children to be anything but "special" and "proud"; and several tenderly poetic children whose inclination was naturally toward the sadness in life.

Sherwood Anderson in his boyhood learned the philosophy of late-nineteenth-century America—work hard, be virtuous, get educated, and success will be inevitable. As he could attend barely into high school, Anderson sought success through hard work and following the usual midwestern dream of city life: after his mother's death in 1895, he left Clyde for Chicago, where he could find only an unpromising warehouse job. Then, with the coming of the Spanish-American War in 1898, Anderson began what would be a series of escapes in his life. He escaped from the warehouse in Chicago by enlisting in the armed forces; and he sought, through attending Wittenberg Academy in 1899–1900, to escape from physical labor through becoming educated. Then his dream of success seemed to be working out.

Anderson became an advertising copywriter in Chicago in 1900, fully accepting the idea of "upward and onward" to financial glory. With his marriage in 1904 to the daughter of a rich Ohio manufacturer and a move in 1906 back to northern Ohio to establish his own mail-order companies, Anderson was becoming highly successful. Unfortunately, his marriage, his growing family, and his business responsibilities brought more worry than pleasure; and late in November, 1912, Anderson made the great legendary escape of his life: he walked out

[4]

of his office, wandered four days over the Ohio countryside in amnesia, recovered his senses, and early in 1913 left alone for Chicago on the quest for satisfaction as an artist.

The Chicago Renaissance in American letters was well under way when Sherwood Anderson joined it in 1913. The middle-aged man was welcomed by those innovative authors who wanted a new vitality in their literature. Anderson became acquainted with such writers as Carl Sandburg, Edgar Lee Masters, Ben Hecht, Margaret Anderson, and Harriet Monroe; and he was accepted into their literary groups not as a new writer but as an experienced if unpublished author, for Anderson had while operating his businesses in Ohio written at least four novels as escape into his imaginative life. These novels he reworked with the advice of his new friends, but without further inspiration nothing good would have come from Sherwood Anderson. Some kind of inspiration came to Anderson when he found the August, 1912, copy of Alfred Stieglitz' Camera Work, which contained Gertrude Stein's experimental prose "Henri Matisse" and "Pablo Picasso." Then, in the winter of 1915–16, he read a copy of Edgar Lee Masters's Spoon River Anthology; and he immediately began his work of genius. Every few nights Anderson sat down to write through a story of a grotesque life in an imaginary town called Winesburg, Ohio. Writing simply and honestly of bittersweet, frustrated lives in Winesburg, Anderson had found his trade, his profession, his way of life for the rest of his days. But success came slowly; even with the publication of Winesburg, Ohio in 1919, only the few knew the sweetness in Sherwood Anderson's stories.

But sometimes the few matter: in June, 1921, the editors of the Dial awarded Anderson a two-thousand-dollar prize for his contributions to American literature in inventing and demonstrating the modern short-story form. The award finally recognized Anderson's merit and pleased him as much as his plan to go to Europe for the first time. On January 20, 1921, his rich New York friend Paul Rosenfeld had telegraphed to offer Anderson and his second wife Tennessee free passage to and from Europe in the spring. On May 14, 1921, the Andersons and Rosenfeld sailed on the French liner Rochambeau. On this trip to Europe, Anderson met, among other literary figures, Ezra Pound, James Joyce, Sylvia Beach—and his daring literary heroine, Gertrude Stein.

Gertrude Stein had, in contrast to Sherwood Anderson, a very fortunate childhood. The last daughter of wealthy parents, Gertrude was born in Allegheny, Pennsylvania, on February 3, 1874. Her early years were spent in Austria, France, Baltimore, Maryland, and Oakland, California. By 1891, both of her parents were dead, and Gertrude Stein escaped from her older brothers' influence by attending Radcliffe College, where she studied psychology under William James. In 1896, she enjoyed her first adult trip to Europe, followed by several years' study at The John Hopkins University School of Medicine. Miss Stein had already determined to follow her own desires in life, and her desire was to study medicine at Hopkins, especially the physiology of the human brain. However, having decided not to complete her work to become a doctor or a medical researcher, she began spending part of her time in Europe, where she was writing fiction by 1903, when she joined her older brother Leo at 27, rue de Fleurus in Paris. Apparently, Miss Stein began writing fiction as self-therapy for problems of disorganization in her life: if she managed to control her fictional characters in their romantic entanglements, perhaps she could create order in her own emotional life.

Gertrude Stein fitted well into the intellectual circles of Paris, especially when her brother Leo led her into stimulating esthetic discussions. In 1904, Gertrude began following Leo's taste in buying modernist paintings; only later would she develop her own exquisite taste in paintings and become personal friends with the great artists. All this time she was creating

[6]

literature (by 1906 Three Lives had been completed), but no one was interested in publishing her writing commercially. In 1907, Gertrude Stein met Alice B. Toklas and started along the path toward independence that was to characterize her life as well as her several later writing styles, for by 1910 Alice and Gertrude were permanent companions; and Alice served to encourage Gertrude to write individualistically and to continue trying to publish her work.

In 1912, Alfred Stieglitz published Gertrude Stein's essays on Matisse and Picasso in Camera Work—the first literary material by Miss Stein to be professionally published. With Alice securely near her and with publication accomplished, Gertrude Stein felt strong enough to separate permanently from her brother in 1913. And then her reputation for writing impenetrably obscure prose was established in 1914, when Tender Buttons appeared. Sherwood Anderson would soon hear of this weird book in Chicago, he would have read her essays in Camera Work, and he would have searched out her privately published Three Lives (1909). But Gertrude Stein knew that she had few enough admirers—indeed few enough readers even willing to understand or try to love her work—and it would be in 1921 before some other, established writer like Sherwood Anderson would appear in her apartment at 27, rue de Fleurus to express his appreciation honestly and sincerely. It was by then important for Sherwood Anderson to say that he admired Gertrude Stein's writing, and it was even more important for Gertrude Stein to be admired.

The first meeting of Gertrude Stein and Sherwood Anderson came about by chance soon after June 13, 1921. In his wandering around Paris, Anderson passed by 8, rue Dupuytren, where the Shakespeare and Company book shop was operated by Miss Sylvia Beach, who later recalled: "One day I noticed an interesting-looking man lingering on the doorstep, his eye caught by a book in the window. The book was Winesburg,

[7]

Ohio, which had recently been published in the United States. Presently he came in and introduced himself as the author. He said he hadn't seen another copy of his book in Paris. I was not surprised, as I had looked everywhere for it myself. . . ."[1] When Anderson hopefully said that he would like to meet Gertrude Stein, Miss Beach generously offered to arrange a meeting by writing:

Dear Miss Gertrude Stein,

Would you let me bring around Mr Sherwood Anderson of Poor White and Winesburg Ohio to see you say tomorrow evening Friday? He is so anxious to know you for he says you have influenced him ever so much & that you stand as such a great master of words.

Unless I hear from you saying NO I will take him to you after dinner to[morrow] night.

Yours affectionately
Sylvia Beach[2]

In an unpublished black notebook of seventy-four pages in which Sherwood Anderson wrote down his impressions of Paris, there is his fresh but unfortunately uncompleted account of this first meeting with Gertrude Stein.

1 "The days were wonderful and the nights were wonderful and the life was pleasant."

"The spoon was set six. Eight was a beginning. It began. Earrings are good to breed. Breed that."[3]

1. Shakespeare and Company (New York: Harcourt, Brace, 1959), p. 30.
2. The Flowers of Friendship: Letters Written to Gertrude Stein, ed. Donald Gallup (New York: Alfred A. Knopf, 1953), pp. 138–39.
3. Anderson tries to quote from memory here and below lines from Gertrude Stein's Tender Buttons (New York: Claire Marie, 1914): "Suppose ear rings, that is one way to breed, breed that" (p. 28); and "Dining is west" (p. 56). Also, he cannot remember the names of some artists whose paintings Miss Stein had collected.

Imagine a strong woman with legs like stone pillars sitting in a room hung thick with Picassos. Formerly there were many Matisses and   too but except 2   these have gone.

The woman is the very symbol of health and strength. She laughs, she smokes cigarettes. She tells stories with an American shrewdness in getting the tang and the kick into the telling.

Gertrude Stein is perhaps 45 and for 10 or perhaps 15 years she has been sitting at a desk in the room writing such sentences as those above. When her first book *Three Lives* was published (at her own expense) and later when *Tender Buttons* appeared a little flame of interest and amusement flared up in America. Newspaper paragraphers quoted her. It became for a time the thing, in smart literary circles, to give readings from her works.

"To dine is west."

A great revolution in the art of words had begun and was being passed over with a laugh.

Gertrude Stein has always been laughed at. Years ago when her work first fell under my eyes and I was startled and profoundly stirred by its significance I made inquiry concerning her. Strange stories came out of Paris. She was a fat woman, very languid, lying on a couch, people came into the room and she stared at them with strange cold eyes. There was a strange power in her by the exercise of which she was able to

Sherwood Anderson returned to the United States, his meeting with Gertrude Stein in Paris having been the high point of his first trip abroad. The friendship was established, and its immediate fruit was Anderson's writing the introduction for Miss Stein's first major anthology.

2

27 Rue de Fleurus
[Fall, 1921]

My dear Anderson

I wonder if you are still interested in doing an essay on me. There is very likely to be a book of mine brought out this winter a collection of short things more or less chronological showing different periods and to be called *Geography and Plays*. There will be portraits too but we don't mention it in the title. It has been suggested that you do an introduction. Of course I would like that because as I told you, you are really the only person who really knows what it is all about. Do let me know what you think about it. Do also please not to forget to send me the books you promised me. I want very much to see them. I have been working a good deal and have had a good summer. I hope your trip ended well. I had more news of you from Marsden Hartley.[4]

Remember me please to Mrs. Anderson

Sincerely yours
Gtde Stein

Presumably, Anderson wrote Miss Stein to accept her invitation to write a preface for Geography and Plays, but his next extant letter introduces a young American writer whom Anderson had met and befriended in Chicago. Ernest Hemingway did not use this note of introduction to meet Gertrude Stein until March, 1922.

4. Marsden Hartley (1877–1943), American painter and poet who studied in Paris and who wrote of Sherwood Anderson in "Spring, 1941," *Story* 19 (September–October 1941): 97–98.

3

Miss Gertrude Stein,
27 Rue de Fleurus,
Paris, France.

Dear Miss Stein:

I am writing this note to make you acquainted with my friend Ernest Hemingway, who with Mrs. Hemingway is going to Paris to live, and will ask him to drop it in the mails when he arrives there.

Mr. Hemingway is an American writer instinctively in touch with everything worthwhile going on here and I know you will find Mr. and Mrs. Hemingway delightful people to know.

They will be at 74 Rue du Cardinal Lemoine.

Sincerely,
Sherwood Anderson

Did you get my note about the introduction? Love to Marsden Hartley.

4

[Paris, January, 1922]

My dear Anderson—

I was caught by a very late summer turning into a very early winter and was consequently laid up awhile and so I did not answer your letter at once and now it's all decided and I hope this finds you the same.

The Four Seas Company of Boston are going to publish my book and the book is to be called *Geography and Plays* and is to be between four and five hundred pages long. It is to be samples of me from 1904 when I wrote *Three Lives* to six months ago. They are xperiments of all kinds I have put on the approximate dates on this table of contents I am sending you. You so thoroughly understand these studies that it is a great pleasure to me to know that you are going to tell about them. I don't see why there should be any aimable limit as to the quantity you are to write. We are hoping at least I am hoping that the Mr. Brown is hoping to put the book out early in the spring and would you communicate directly with him about the preface. I am suggesting this just to save time. While I was laid up I worked a lot and I have done two plays which are I think quite what plays should be but they are not included in the book because they were not ready. Perhaps you will be over this summer again and as [an] Arab remarked to us about the possibility of tram ways in Tangiers that would be nice.

Thanks so much for your book *The Egg*. I like "The Egg."[5] The good part of your work is that it is direct. Most of the realistic work of America is translated one does not quite know from what or where but it is a translation. Perhaps it's Zola and they don't know it. Perhaps it isn't. Anyway you have brains valuable brains that translate into style conception. You are not among the muck of them who crying give them liberty or give me death when you give them liberty give you death. But anyhow it's alright and I am looking forward very genuinely to the new novel. Do tell Mrs Anderson that we were awfully pleased with she worked her way through college.

I guess that's all just now. I can only repeat that I have never had more genuine emotion than when you came and understood me and it is a great delight to me to know that it is you who is to present me. *Presentez moi* as they say in French. Do let me as well as Mr. Brown of the Four Seas Pub-

5. Miss Stein refers to "The Egg" in Anderson's *The Triumph of the Egg* (New York: B. W. Huebsch, 1921), pp. 46–63.

lication Company 168 Dartmouth St. Boston hear from you soon

Always yours
Gtde Stein

5

708 Royal Street
New Orleans
[February, 1922]

My dear Gertrude Stein—

I was delighted to get your letter of today and to hear that arrangements are made for the publication of the book.

I was afraid you might have changed your mind about having me write the introduction and had you done so I should have been quite upset. It's a literary job I'd rather do than any other I know of. I'll get at it very soon and send it along. Someone told me you were off Americans, that you had become bored with them and that frightened me too. "I'll bet she'll put me in with the rest of the mess and chuck us all," I thought.

In the January Dial Paul Rosenfeld had an article on my own work in which he spoke of the influence on myself of first coming across one of your books, at the time they [were] raising such a guffa over here. I'd like you to see the article but haven't it here.[6]

I came down here about a month ago and am living in the old French Creole quarter, the most civilized place I've found

---

6. Paul Rosenfeld, "Sherwood Anderson," *Dial* 72 (January 1922): 29–42: "The man's feeling for words, present always in him, re-enforced one casual day when someone, expecting to produce a raw haha, showed him the numbers of Camera Work containing Gertrude Stein's essays on Matisse, Picasso, and Mable Dodge, is here [in *Winesburg, Ohio*] mature" (p. 37).

in America, and have been writing like a man gone mad ever since I got off the train.

You will hear from me with the introduction very soon.

Your Sincere Admirer.

Sherwood Anderson

6

[New Orleans, February, 1922]

Dear Gertrude Stein—

Here it is. I could write a volume and not in the end say more.

I hope you'll like it.

Sherwood Anderson

Permanent address
Critchfield & Company
Brooks Bldg.,
Chicago.

7 THE WORK OF GERTRUDE STEIN

One evening in the winter, some years ago, my brother came to my rooms in the city of Chicago bringing with him a book by Gertrude Stein. The book was called *Tender Buttons* and, just at that time, there was a good deal of fuss and fun being made over it in American newspapers. I had already read a book of Miss Stein's called *Three Lives* and had thought it contained some of the best writing ever done by an American. I was curious about this new book.

My brother had been at some sort of a gathering of literary people on the evening before and someone had read aloud from Miss Stein's new book. The party had been a success. After a few lines the reader stopped and was greeted by loud shouts of laughter. It was generally agreed that the author had done a thing we Americans call "putting something across" —the meaning being that she had, by a strange freakish performance, managed to attract attention to herself, get herself discussed in the newspapers, become for a time a figure in our hurried, harried lives.

My brother, as it turned out, had not been satisfied with the explanation of Miss Stein's work then current in America, and so he bought *Tender Buttons* and brought it to me, and we sat for a time reading the strange sentences. "It gives words an oddly new intimate flavor and at the same time makes familiar words seem almost like strangers, doesn't it," he said. What my brother did, you see, was to set my mind going on the book, and then, leaving it on the table, he went away.

And now, after these years, and having sat with Miss Stein by her own fire in the rue de Fleurus in Paris I am asked to write something by way of an introduction to a new book she is about to issue.

As there is in America an impression of Miss Stein's personality, not at all true and rather foolishly romantic, I would like first of all to brush that aside. I had myself heard stories of a long dark room with a languid woman lying on a couch, smoking cigarettes, sipping absinthes perhaps and looking out upon the world with tired, disdainful eyes. Now and then she rolled her head slowly to one side and uttered a few words, taken down by a secretary who approached the couch with trembling eagerness to catch the falling pearls.

You will perhaps understand something of my own surprise and delight when, after having been fed up on such tales and rather Tom Sawyerishly hoping they might be true, I was taken to her to find instead of this languid impossibility a woman of striking vigor, a subtle and powerful mind, a discrimination in the arts such as I have found in no other American born man or woman, and a charmingly brilliant conversationalist.

"Surprise and delight" did I say? Well, you see, my feeling is something like this. Since Miss Stein's work was first brought to my attention I have been thinking of it as the most important pioneer work done in the field of letters in my time. The loud guffaws of the general that must inevitably follow the bringing forward of more of her work do not irritate me but I would like it if writers, and particularly young writers, would come to understand a little what she is trying to do and what she is in my opinion doing.

My thought in the matter is something like this—that every artist working with words as his medium, must at times be profoundly irritated by what seems the limitations of his medium. What things does he not wish to create with words! There is the mind of the reader before him and he would like to create in that reader's mind a whole new world of sensations, or rather one might better say he would like to call back into life all of the dead and sleeping senses.

There is a thing one might call "the extension of the province of his art" one wants to achieve. One works with words and one would like words that have a taste on the lips, that have a perfume to the nostrils, rattling words one can throw into a box and shake, making a sharp, jingling sound, words that, when seen on the printed page, have a distinct arresting effect upon the eye, words that when they jump out from under the pen one may feel with the fingers as one might caress the cheeks of his beloved.

And what I think is that these books of Gertrude Stein's do in a very real sense recreate life in words.

We writers are, you see, all in such a hurry. There are such grand things we must do. For one thing the Great American Novel must be written and there is the American or English Stage that must be uplifted by our very important contributions, to say nothing of the epic poems, sonnets to my lady's eyes, and what not. We are all busy getting these grand and important thoughts and emotions into the pages of printed books.

And in the meantime the little words, that are the soldiers with which we great generals must make our conquests, are neglected.

There is a city of English and American words and it has been a neglected city. Strong broad shouldered words, that should be marching across open fields under the blue sky, are clerking in little dusty dry goods stores, young virgin words are being allowed to consort with whores, learned words have been put to the ditch digger's trade. Only yesterday I saw a word that once called a whole nation to arms serving in the mean capacity of advertising laundry soap.

For me the work of Gertrude Stein consists in a rebuilding, an entire new recasting of life, in the city of words. Here is one artist who has been able to accept ridicule, who has even forgone the privilege of writing the great American novel, uplifting our English speaking stage, and wearing the bays of the great poets, to go live among the little housekeeping words, the swaggering bullying street-corner words, the honest working, money saving words, and all the other forgotten and neglected citizens of the sacred and half forgotten city.

Would it not be a lovely and charmingly ironic gesture of the gods if, in the end, the work of this artist were to prove the most lasting and important of all the word slingers of our generation!

8

27 Rue de Fleurus
[March, 1922]

My dear Sherwood,

I am very much touched and more than delighted with the preface. It is just what it should be but then I knew it would be. I really cannot tell you how pleased I am with it. Don't you ever believe what they tell you about me. I never am off Americans on the contrary I am all for my compies which is short for compatriots and anyway you are special. Besides there are the Hemingways you sent and they are charming. He is a delightful fellow and I like his talk and I am teaching him to cut his wife's hair. He can learn to do it so much better than the barber. We have had a good time with them and hope to see more of them. And how about you and Mrs Anderson. Aren't you coming over too again. It's getting on to spring now and that's when the old Americans leave and the new Americans come. We would like you either way. I hope my publisher hasn't bothered you too much. I am sending the preface to him and he'll get it in plenty of time so don't worry to make another copy. I am sending this to your permanent address which is very nearly permanently illisible as the French say with this kind of an address when they don't copy it but the "trembling secretary" and I did a solid concentration and the light came, I hope it came rightly. Anyway a thousand thanks and much love, our best respects to Mrs. Anderson.

                                        Yours
                                        Gtde Stein.

[18]

9

Miss Gertrude Stein,
27 Rue de Fleurus
Paris, France.

My dear Gertrude Stein:
Of course, I understand what you said about your disliking Americans was only fun. I am delighted that you are delighted with the preface. Anyway, I knew what I wrote was sincerely felt. I have no doubt but that the Four Seas will get it as I sent it some time ago.

I had a charming letter from Mr. Hemingway, stating how glad he is to know you. I, myself, will not get to France this year, although the Lord knows I would like to be there this Spring.

With love

Yours very sincerely,
Sherwood Anderson

10

New York,
Monday August 14 [19]22

My Dear Gertrude Stein—
I am delighted with the photograph and with the delightful memories it awakes in me. I am quite sure the appearance of your new book over here will arouse a good deal of discussion. As to whether it will arouse anything else I can't say. It hasn't come to me yet but I am looking forward to its coming

eagerly. The Four Seas Company promised to send it as soon as it is off the press.

I am in New York at work. Since I left New Orleans in March have done nothing that is worth a damn. Now I am working again. Whether this is a real start or not I can't say yet.

The *Dial* bought my new book—the one I wrote in New Orleans—for serial publication so it will not be out in book form until sometime in the spring.[7] I think it is pretty good. The first long thing I've done that sticks together and doesn't break to pieces anywhere. Now I am flirting with a new long book and have made two or three false starts at it. When it gets going under my hand I'll be a decent citizen again.

Meanwhile I am here, in the apartment of a friend whose family have gone away for the summer. Have run away from all my friends, including friend wife, and am fiddling about at the job.

Next year, if I have any luck or any money will go to Europe again. Perhaps I will go to Italy or Spain this time but, no matter where I go, I'll probably have a look in at Paris at you.

With Love.
Sherwood Anderson

c/o B. W. Huebsch
116—E 13th St.
New York.

7. Anderson's novel *Many Marriages* (New York: B. W. Huebsch, 1923) was serialized in the *Dial* from October, 1922, through March, 1923.

11

New York
Aug. 21 [1922]

Dear Gertrude Stein—

In the New York *Tribune* here yesterday there appeared a glib and meaningless thing by Burton Rascoe supposed to be a record of something said about your work by myself, something in explanation of your work.[8] There was a conversation about your work between Edmund Wilson and myself. I recognize little I said in this glib and trite transcript of it. I want you to know I deny any responsibility. That's all.

After all a writer does care about the printed word and a thing of this sort, carelessly thrown together and then put into your mouth, makes cold shivers run down the back.

Sincerely.
Sherwood Anderson

12

[Paris, September, 1922]

My dear Sherwood

I liked hearing from you again but I don't like to have you troubled. I haven't as a matter of fact seen the *Tribune* but there is one thing of which you can be certain, I will never misunderstand you or your understanding of me. I don't think you quite realise what it means to have some one and you have been the only one quite simply understand what it is all about simply understand as any one would suppose everyone would understand and to so charmingly and directly tell it to me.

8. Burton Rascoe (1892–1957), literary editor of the *New York Tribune* after January, 1922; the column mentioning Anderson and Stein was "A Bookman's Day Book: August 9," *New York Tribune*, 20 August 1922.

I am glad to hear about your new book. What is its name. I like a name. I wish you were with us we are spending a month at St. Rémy a nice little provincial Provence town I think you would find it as nice as New Orleans. I have been working a lot, a sort of White Melanctha which I have called, "Why are there Whites to Console." And I have just done a nice one a little one I like very much "Prudence Caution and foresight, A story of Avignon."[9] It's rather nice—about a valet in a hotel. Anyway do write from time to time even if it's only a note. I like to hear from you. Best to Mrs. Anderson.

Yours
Gertrude Stein

13

12 St. Luke's Place
New York
Sept. 22 [19]22

Dear Gertrude Stein—

Have had an adventurous summer. In the first place I was in Chicago for months and was no good. Wrote nothing worth a snap of the finger. So I got me a second hand Ford and spent some weeks going to the races on country race tracks. I have a great fondness for American toughs and that's the place to find them on every bush.

Afterward I decided, or rather we decided, that Tennessee Mitchell and I were not doing the job of being a man and wife very well so we called it off. However that isn't being advertised, not yet.

The new novel is called *Many Marriages*. I think you'll like

9. "Why Are There Whites to Console: A History in Three Parts," in *As Fine as Melanctha* (1914–1930), foreword by Natalie Clifford Barney (New Haven: Yale University Press, 1954), pp. 198–218; "Prudence Caution and Foresight, A Story of Avignon," in *A Novel of Thank You*, introduction by Carl Van Vechten (New Haven: Yale University Press, 1958), pp. 253–57.

it pretty well. It will be out in book form in February and I'll send you one at once.

Have written an article about you, Paul Rosenfeld, Ring Lardner and Sinclair Lewis for New Republic but do not know whether they will take it or not. If they do I will send it on to you.

Have fallen in love, am living in New York, am writing again and am planning and trying to save money to go to Europe early next year. Want to go to Italy but want also to see Paris and you in passing. It's a question of whether I get together money enough but perhaps I will.

Have got to raise enough to take both my lady love and myself as America is no place for lovers so am going to work hard as the devil for a while.

Lots of Love.
Sherwood Anderson

Anderson's "new love" was Elizabeth Prall, to whom he was unhappily married from 1924 to 1932. The article was his "Four American Impressions: Gertrude Stein, Paul Rosenfeld, Ring Lardner, Sinclair Lewis," New Republic, 11 October 1922, pp. 171–73.

14 FROM "FOUR AMERICAN IMPRESSIONS"

One who thinks a great deal about people and what they are up to in the world comes inevitably in time to relate them to experiences connected with one's own life. The round, hard apples in this old orchard are the breasts of my beloved. The curved, round hill in the distance is the body of my beloved, lying asleep. One cannot avoid practising this trick of lifting people out of the spots on which in actual life they stand and transferring them to what seems at the moment some more fitting spot in one's fanciful world.

And one gets also a kind of aroma from people. They are green, healthy, growing things or they have begun to decay. There is something in this man, to whom I have just talked, that has sent me away from him smiling and in an odd way pleased with myself. Why has this other man, although his words were kindly and his deeds apparently good, spread a cloud over my sky?

In my own boyhood in an Ohio town I went about delivering newspapers at kitchen doors, and there were certain houses to which I went—old brick houses with immense old-fashioned kitchens—in which I loved to linger. On Saturday mornings I sometimes managed to collect a fragrant cooky at such a place, but there was something else that held me. Something got into my mind connected with the great, light kitchens and the women working in them that came sharply back when, last year, I went to visit an American woman, Miss Gertrude Stein, in her own large room in the house at 27 rue de Fleurus in Paris. In the great kitchen of my fanciful world in which I have, ever since that morning, seen Miss Stein standing, there is a most sweet and gracious aroma. Along the walls are many shining pots and pans, and there are innumerable jars of fruits, jellies and preserves. Something is going on in the great room, for Miss Stein is a worker in words with the same loving touch in her strong fingers that was characteristic of the women of the kitchens of the brick houses in the town of my boyhood. She is an American woman of the old sort, one who cares for the handmade goodies and who scorns the factory-made foods, and in her own great kitchen she is making something with her materials, something sweet to the tongue and fragrant to the nostrils.

That her materials are the words of our English speech and that we do not, most of us, know or care too much what she is up to does not greatly matter to me. The impression I wish now to give you of her is of one very intent and earnest in a matter most of us have forgotten. She is laying word against word, relating sound to sound, feeling for the taste, the smell, the rhythm of the individual word. She is attempting to do something for the writers of our English speech that may be better understood after a time, and she is not in a hurry. And one has always that picture of the woman in the great kitchen of words, standing there by a table, clean, strong, with red cheeks and sturdy legs, always quietly and smilingly at work. If her smile has in it something of the mystery, to the male at least, of the Mona Lisa, I remember that the women in the kitchens on the wintry mornings wore often that same smile.

She is making new, strange and to my ears sweet combinations of words. As an American writer I admire her because she, in her person, represents something sweet and healthy in our American life, and because I have a kind of undying faith that what she is up to in her word kitchen in Paris is of more importance to writers of English than the work of many of our more easily understood and more widely accepted word artists.

15

12 St. Luke's Place
Sept. 30 [1922]
New York.

Dear Friend—

I am taking the liberty of giving a note to you to an American girl in Europe—Miss Lois Wright. She is alive and charming and wants a bit of help in the way of meeting some of the painters.

Believe me, dear friend, I'll not make you a harbor for tourists but if you see Miss Wright you'll like her.

With Love.
Sherwood Anderson

16

Miss Gertrude Stein
27 Rue de Fleurus.

Dear Gertrude Stein,
   This note will introduce Miss Lois Wright—the American girl about whom I wrote you. Will you not see her and help her all you can? She is ambitious and talented. Any trouble you may take will be worthwhile.

> With Love.
> Sherwood Anderson.

17

27 Rue de Fleurus
[April, 1923]

My dear Sherwood
   I have been xpecting to hear from you for this long time and I haven't and now here is your book.[10] Thanks so much for it. I have just finished reading it and this is what I think. It's a fine piece of work and has in it some writing that I find far better than anything you have done before. Particularly the description of the man when he goes to Chicago and has his girl in the ordinary way. Frankly I think that almost comes up to the description of a similar thing in Samuel Johnson which has always been to me a master-piece also I think you are right when you say that it is a big advance on your other long things in that it does not fall to pieces, it does not fall to pieces nor does it hold together artificially, on the other hand there is to

10. Miss Stein refers to *Many Marriages*, published on February 20, 1923.

[26]

my thinking a little too much tendency to make the finale come too frequently that is to say you the writer know a little too frequently that there is an ending. May I say that there should be a beginning a middle and an ending, and you have a tendency to make it a beginning an ending an ending and an ending. Then there is perhaps a little bit too much tendency to mix yourself and the hero together, it is a little your weakness in your long things, you do a little tend to find yourself more interesting than your hero and you tend to put yourself in his place. You don't at all with your short things but you always have somewhat with your long things. On the other hand though your short things in this respect are better than your long things there is infinitely better finer and truer writing in your long things. You need the longer form actually to produce your best of that I am convinced. This long one is an enormous step in advance for you, your writing here has an amplitude and very often a completion that you have never gotten before. It rises and spreads, and when it does not flow I think it is always due to the fault I mention that you feel yourself more than your creation, if you master that weakness you will rise to very great heights because I tell you honestly Sherwood and this is straight you are the best writing America does and you are in the great tradition.

Did you get our book I sent you with the valentine, I sent the valentines including yours to the *Little Review*. Do let me hear from you soon. We are back in Paris now for keeps and it would be awfully nice to see you here. I have been doing a fair amount of work since I have been home.

Do write

Yours
Gtde Stein

Gertrude Stein's first writing about Sherwood Anderson was her superbly confusing "Idem the Same—A Valentine to Sherwood Anderson," Little Review 9 (Spring 1923): 5–9.

18 IDEM THE SAME
A VALENTINE TO SHERWOOD ANDERSON

I knew too that through them I knew too that he was through, I knew too that he threw them, I knew too that they were through, I knew too I knew too, I knew I knew them.

I knew to them.

If they tear a hunter through, if they tear through a hunter, if they tear through a hunt and a hunter, if they tear through the different sizes of the six, the different sizes of the six which are these, a woman with a white package under one arm and a black package under the other arm and dressed in brown with a white blouse, the second Saint Joseph the third a hunter in a blue coat and black garters and a plaid cap, a fourth a knife grinder who is full faced and a very little woman with black hair and a yellow hat and an excellently smiling appropriate soldier. All these as you please.

In the meantime examples of the same lily. In this way please have you rung.

What Do I See

A very little snail.
A medium-sized turkey.
A small band of sheep.
A fair orange tree.
All nice wives are like that.
Listen to them from here.
Oh.
You did not have an answer.
Here.
Yes,

A Very Valentine

Very fine is my valentine.
Very fine and very mine.
Very mine is my valentine very mine and very fine.
Very fine is my valentine and mine, very fine very mine
and mine is my valentine.

Why Do You Feel Differently

Why do you feel differently about a very little snail and
a big one,
Why do you feel differently about a medium-sized
turkey and a very large one.
Why do you feel differently about a small band of
sheep and several sheep that are riding.
Why do you feel differently about a fair orange tree and
one that has blossoms as well.

Oh, very well.
All nice wives are like that.
To Be
No Please.
To Be
They can please
Not to be
Do they please.
Not to be
Do they not please
Yes please.
Do they please.
No please.
Do they not please
NO please.
Do they please.
Please.

If you please.
And if you please
And if they please
And they please.
To be pleased
Not to be pleased.
Not to be displeased.
To be pleased and to please.

Kneeling

One two three four five six seven eight nine and ten.

The tenth is a little one kneeling and giving away a rooster with this feeling.

I have mentioned one, four five seven eight and nine.

Two is also giving away an animal.

Three is changed as to disposition.

Six is in question if we mean mother and daughter, black and black caught her, and she offers to be three she offers it to me.

That is very right and should come out below and just so.

Bundles For Them
A History of Giving Bundles

We were able to notice that each one in a way carried a bundle, they were not a trouble to them nor were they all bundles as some of them were chickens some of them pheasants some of them sheep and some of them bundles, they were not a trouble to them and then indeed we learned that it was the principal recreation and they were so arranged that they were not given away, and to-day they were given away.

I will not look at them again.

They will not look for them again.

They have not seen them here again.

They are in there and we hear them again.

In which way are stars brighter than they are. When we have come to this decision. We mention many thousands of buds. And when I close my eyes I see them.

If you hear her snore
It is not before you love her
You love her so that to be her beau is very lovely
She is sweetly there and her curly hair is very lovely
She is sweetly here and I am very near and that is very lovely.

She is my tender sweet and her little feet are stretched out well which is a treat and very lovely.

Her little tender nose is between her little eyes which close and are very lovely.

She is very lovely and mine which is very lovely.

On Her Way

If you can see why she feels that she kneels if you can see why he knows that he shows what he bestows, if you can see why they share what they share, need we question that there is no doubt that by this time if they had intended to come they would have sent some notice of such intention. She and they and indeed the decision itself is not early dissatisfaction.

In This Way

Keys please, it is useless to alarm any one it is useless to alarm some one it is useless to be alarming and to get fertility in gardens in salads in heliotrope and in dishes. Dishes and wishes are mentioned and dishes and wishes are not capable of darkness. We like sheep. And so does he.

Let Us Describe

Let us describe how they went. It was a very windy night and the road although in excellent condition and extremely well graded has many turnings and although the curves are not sharp the rise is considerable. It was a very windy night and some of the larger vehicles found it more prudent not to venture. In consequence some of those who had planned to go were unable to do so. Many others did go and there was a sacrifice, of what shall we, a sheep, a hen, a cock, a village, a ruin, and all that and then that having been blessed let us bless it.

19

[Reno, spring, 1923]

Miss Gertrude Stein

Dear Friend—

Got your note yesterday and just recently have been thinking about you a good deal. You see, in this book, on which I am at work, I am trying to make a kind of picture of the artist's life in the midst of present day American life.[11] It has been a job. So much to discard. Have never thrown away so much stuff. I want to make it a sort of tale you see, not a preachment.

Also I have to find out if I can what really affected the fellow. There isn't any doubt about you there. It was a vital day for me when I stumbled upon you.

But also there was and is something else. There was not only your work but also your room in the house there in Paris. That was something special too. I mean the effect on myself. You would be surprised to know just how altogether American I found you.

You see, dear friend, I believe in this damn mixed-up coun-

11. *A Story Teller's Story* (New York: B. W. Huebsch, 1924).

try of ours. In an odd way I'm in love with it. And you get into it, in my sense of it, quite tremendously.

I'm here checking over things and people that have meant most. You, Jane Heap, Dreiser, Paul Rosenfeld, Van Wyck Brooks, Alfred Stieglitz, that about nails the list.[12] It is a list that would make Jane sputter with wrath perhaps. She's an arbitrary one—that same Jane.

What I have to figure is just the people who have given me fine moments. I've an idea that's what counts most.

Well you'll see the book someday. I'm glad Jane is going to publish the "Valentine." I like it because it always stirs me and is full of sharp critcism too.

Am sitting right here in a desert as big as God until I get this book done and a divorce. Then I'll shift to something else and I hope some of these days my shifting will bring me to your door again.

> With Love.
> Sherwood

20

[Reno, November, 1923]

Dear Gertrude Stein—

Here is a long and involved letter from my publisher proposing a somewhat involved plan to be worked out by a lady I do not know too well—believe I once dined with her.[13]

12. Jane Heap (?–1964) and Margaret Anderson (1893–?) founded and published *The Little Review* in Chicago in 1914 and moved it to Paris in 1924; Van Wyck Brooks (1886–1963), critic and interpreter of American literary history; Anderson dedicated *A Story Teller's Story* to Alfred Stieglitz (1864–1946), a New York photographer and enthusiast of modern painting.

13. On November 8, 1923, B. W. Huebsch wrote Sherwood Anderson that he was thinking of publishing a volume of short stories, with introduction and linking material, to be prepared by Miss Frances Newman of Atlanta, who was a book reviewer. The book was to include one story by Sherwood Anderson and perhaps one by Gertrude Stein. Huebsch asked Anderson to mention the proposal to Miss Stein.

I myself have written Ben Huebsch to go ahead as far as I am concerned.

I have no doubt you will understand the purpose as well as I do and will take a chance—as I am doing.

Will you write Ben Huebsch about it?

I asked Huebsch to send you the new book of tales—*Horses and Men*—and it should be along to you about the time this note gets to you.[14]

Are you well? Are you at work? I have got off my new long book which I have decided I shall call *A Story Teller's Story*. One of the magazines may publish part of it.[15]

Now I am again at some shorter things—the one at present on the rack being rather pure fun.

Am still in the far west but dream perhaps I may have shekels enough to get to Europe & Paris next year. It would be fun to see you again.

Sherwood Anderson

21

[Reno]
May 9—1923

Dear Gertrude Stein—

Your letter found me out yesterday. Am still out in the far west—in the desert country—and I surely did think I had written you recently. There might be a letter—somewhere—on the road to you.

I got the book—with the charming valentine— about two weeks ago—someone forwarded it.

And now I have this letter of yours about the book.

Do you know I think it the most clear-headed criticism I've

14. *Horses and Men* was published by Huebsch on October 26, 1923.
15. Two installments of *A Story Teller's Story* were published in *Phantasmus* 1 (May 1924): 1–37; and 1 (June 1924): 109–64. A third section appeared in *Century* 108 (August 1924): 489–96.

had and that you have its weaknesses and good points about rightly sized up.

It's a job—for an American—with the damned Anglo-Saxon blood in him, to become quite impersonal, but I've a hope I'm going toward it.

I cut out of New York about the time your book and my own were published and did not see the comments on either.

I felt like work and wanted to work and did not want to be thinking much about the job done—for good or evil.

Then I got out here and the painting impulse got me and I've been fairly swimming.

For one thing I'm doing a quite frankly autobiographical book—(that may take something of the tendency to be too much interested in self out of me)—unload it—as it were.

Then I am getting a book of tales—call it *Horses and Men*—ready for book publication this fall. There are, I fancy, some good things in it.

I am dead set on getting to Paris next year and do hope I shall make it and that you will be there. If you aren't I'll look you up—where you are.

I believe I'm getting something in painting. I get up early —write in the morning—tear around for two or three hours and then settle down to paint. It excites me, even more than writing—it's such a holy gamble—for me anyway.

I've a long novel at work in me but I shall not get to that until next fall or winter.

Am delighted you are working. I fancy, what you are doing means more to more people than you know.

With Love.
Sherwood.

22

My dear Sherwood,

How goes it, haven't heard from you for some time. Now that spring is a little in the air I am beginning to wonder if you are coming along soon it isn't all spring yet but there are signs. How is the book, is it getting on. Hemingway is just back, he saw Jane Heap in New York and thus indirectly I had news of you. He seems very much not to have liked Canada. It's nice having them back. I am inclosing a little skit I presented to him on going away and which may amuse you. I have just done a medium sized thing, "Wherein the South differs from the North," which quite pleases me. I am also at work on a birth-day book which Picasso is to illustrate.[16] As soon as it's done I will send it to you. Do let me learn more about yourself and everything and what your plans are

Always
Gtde Stein

23

[Reno, March, 1924]

My Dear Gertrude Stein—

How very good to hear from you and the news of the birth-day book. We'll be looking for it. I had a new thing in the February Mercury—I would like you to see but I have no copy here. Perhaps it will appear in one of the bookstores there.

16. Miss Stein's "skit" for Hemingway was "He and They, Heming-way: A Portrait," Ex Libris 1 (December 1923): 192. She also refers to "Wherein the South differs from the North," in Useful Knowledge (New York: Payson & Clarke, 1928), pp. 19–37; and "A Birthday Book," in Alphabets and Birthdays, introduction by Donald Gallup (New Haven: Yale University Press, 1957), pp. 127–54.

The new Mercury—Mencken-Nathan is about what you might expect.[17]

Lordy I'd like to see Hemingway and his lady. When you see him tell him I finally got the angle on the Chicago * * * thing and that it gave me a bad case of fantods. Life has some sweet angles.[18]

There is a book by an American negro—Jean Toomer—called Cane I would like you to see. Real color and splash—no fake negro this time, I'm sure. Do look it up—Boni & Liveright.[19]

Have been sick for a month and very little done—an incomplete novel piled on my desk in confusion. Am still in the mountains but will leave here in about a month and spend April and May on the coast. Little chance for Europe this year. Haven't got the price. Might make some by lecturing (the Americans, as you know, having a bug on lectures) but have always drawn back from the damn foolishness. Won't do it unless I have to.

Have a good intricate theme for this novel and hope to make it march when I get out of here.

Word is that the French will finally publish Winesburg this year but I hardly believe it. It's Gallimard and you know how fast he is.[20] Would like to see good old Jane Heap and M[argaret] Anderson but will probably not be in New York until fall. May spend the summer in New Orleans. Will get to

17. H. L. Mencken (1880–1956) and George Jean Nathan (1882–1958) together edited the Smart Set from 1908 and 1914 respectively to 1923; then in 1924 they founded the American Mercury, in which Anderson published a section of A Story Teller's Story, "Caught," 1 (February 1924): 165–76.

18. Anderson refers to a case of adultery and murder which he describes in Sherwood Anderson's Memoirs: A Critical Edition, edited by Ray Lewis White (Chapel Hill: University of North Carolina Press, 1969), pp. 429–31.

19. Jean Toomer, Cane, foreword by Waldo Frank (New York: Boni & Liveright, 1923).

20. The first French translation of Winesburg, Ohio was Winesburg-en-Ohio, trans. Marguerite Gay (Paris: Gallimard, 1927).

Paris again one of these days—first time a good windfall comes my way.

My love to the Hemingways.

Sherwood Anderson.

To be sure—
c/o B. W. Huebsch,
116 W–13th St.
New York City.

24.

[Belley, September 8, 1924]

Sherwood Anderson
c/o B. W. Huebsch
116 W 13 St
New York

Dear Sherwood,

Miss [?] has just sent me a letter but alas we are not in Paris but I am looking forward to her being there when I get back so that I can have some first hand information about you, but do write to me in any case you know how very much I like to know what's happening to you. Had a very good time with Jane Heap in Paris who is writing up a long article and possibly a book on me. Am having a vacation very quaint and rather wonderful as far as eating and landscape is concerned, landscape is getting into my "Birth and Marriage"[21] at which I am writing hard but then neither landscapes nor eating can do that any harm best to you always

Gtde Stein.

21. Published in *Alphabets and Birthdays*, pp. 175–98.

[38]

25

Dear Gertrude Stein—

It was good to get your card. I have been writing hard. About a month or six weeks ago I suddenly started off into a novel and have been going it ever since. I think I shall call it "Love and War." It is a somewhat different sort of thing than I have ever tried before—the people more sophisticated. Now I should say it is about two thirds done.

When I came down here with my wife it was ungodly hot but now the days are charming and I always have been rather charmed with this country. It isn't so damned progressive as the rest of the country, more easy walking. The nigger I dare say has a lot to do with that. I like the black men, the way they walk talk work and laugh. Well enough I remember the first thing of yours I read—in the *Three Lives*—about the nigger woman. Why it hasn't been included in some of the lists of great short stories I don't know.

In about two weeks I should be able to send you a copy of my *Story Teller's Story*—my book this year.

Going to Paris depends altogether on luck.

By the way I have a seventeen year old son—Bob Anderson —in Europe now. He has worked his way over on a freight boat and perhaps will not get to Paris. He's a charming lad. Wants to be a painter. If he ever comes your way I'll tell him to call on you.

Wish I could see Jane. She's a dandy—one of the real personalities I've met. Is she staying in Paris? I've been out of New York for two years now but will go there this winter.

If I make any money at any time you will see me again in Paris. Lordy I'd like it. When you have anything new do let me see it and tell Jane to let me see the book on you.

Lots of Love.

Sherwood Anderson

I am going to ask a young American admirer of yours—Mr. Whitney Wells—to come in and see you. He is at the Hotel D'Alsace—rue des Beaux Arts.

A Story Teller's Story, the first of Sherwood Anderson's three autobiographies, was published by B. W. Huebsch on October 15, 1924. The following passages about Gertrude Stein are reprinted from A Story Teller's Story: A Critical Text, *ed. Ray Lewis White (Cleveland: Press of Case Western Reserve University, 1968), pp. 260–61, 263, 271–72.*

26   FROM A Story Teller's Story

How significant words had become to me. At about this time an American woman living in Paris—Miss Gertrude Stein—had published a book called *Tender Buttons* and it had come into my hands. How it had excited me. Here was something purely experimental and dealing in words separated from sense—in the ordinary meaning of the word sense—an approach I was sure the poets must often be compelled to make. Was it an approach that would help me? I decided to try it. . . .

I had come to Gertrude Stein's book about which everyone laughed but about which I did not laugh. It excited me as one might grow excited in going into a new and wonderful country where everything is strange—a sort of Lewis and Clark expedition for me. Here were words laid before me as the painter had laid the color pans on the table in my presence. My mind did a kind of jerking flop and after Miss Stein's book had come into my hands I spent days going about with a tablet of paper in my pocket and making new and strange combinations of words. The result was I thought a new familiarity with the words of my own vocabulary. I became a little conscious where before I had been unconscious. Perhaps it was then I really fell in love with words, wanted to give each word I used every chance to show itself at its best. . . .

I had a penchant for taking my own life rather seriously. Americans in general pretended their own lives did not matter. They were continually talking of devoting their lives to business, to some reform, to their children, to the public. I had been called a Modern and perhaps only deserved the title inasmuch as I was a born questioner. I did not take such words people were always saying too seriously. Often enough I used to lie on my bed in my room and on moonlight nights I lit a cigarette and spent some time looking at myself. I lifted up my legs, one after the other, and rejoiced at the thought that they might yet take me into many strange places. Then I lifted my arms and looked long and earnestly at my hands. Why had they not served me better? Why would they not serve me better? It was easy enough to put a pen into the fingers. I myself was perfectly willing to be a great author. Why would not the pen slide more easily and gracefully over the paper? What sentences I wanted to write, what paragraphs, what pages! If reading Miss Stein had given me a new sense of my own limited vocabulary, had made me feel words as more living things, if seeing the work of many of the modern painters had given me a new feeling for form and color, why would my own hands not become better servants to me?

27

27 Rue de Fleurus
[November, 1924]

My dear Sherwood,

That faithless Huebsch did not send me your book but I have gotten hold of it anyway and I am delighted delighted delighted, it is just what I have hoped and xpected you would do a whole book done with the whole of you head and all and sustained all the way through and it's pretty good to be sustained all through a whole long book. As writing it's far and away the best you have ever done as good as the "Story of the Egg" and simpler more matured and mellower. I can't tell you what of it I liked best. To begin with the Fenimore Cooper business is almost the best piece of writing I know, then about your father and about your birth and Nora, Nora and that whale business for simplicity and absolute marriage between words movement and image is perhaps the best, the little about horses, the only thing to compare with it at all is George Borrow, *Lavengro*, and yours has the simpler direction of to-day and in quality it's as good, we are simpler and you have wonderfully done it, then all the little bits the description of movie actors and oil, they are all gems, well Sherwood all I can say is that it is the first time since the "Story of the Egg" that I am satisfied, and as I am not easily satisfied I hope you are pleased that I am satisfied, I am, I am satisfied and I am pleased to be satisfied. There is all through this book possession instead of possessed, anyway do some more. I am awfully touched by what you say of me but you know that your feeling about my work is more precious to me than that of any one else, well I am sure now you have come into your own. I am looking forward to the next one. Please give my greetings to your wife, I like you so much and I like what you have done so much I will surely like her as much too. I hope it will turn out to be a near best seller and that you will be coming over next year and we will see each other again. I have not yet met Whitney Wells we were out of town and then he was out of town but I am seeing him this evening. I am working a lot at present rather obsessed with tenses, doing a long thing beside short ones, but more of that later, once more lots of love and much pleasure in it

Yours

Gtde Stein.

28

Dear Gertrude Stein

I am back at home—540–B St. Peter Street, New Orleans—back with the niggers, the ships, the old houses, the rich—often rank—southern smells I love.

Am working again—the pen flying. I lectured, I saw people —Stieglitz, Rosenfeld, Jane (for just a moment), that woman who had the letter from you about raising money for the Marne house—McBride[22]—a lot of people you know.

I am to write the blurb for the cover of Hemingway's book. I liked his stories—all of them.[23]

Made a little money and often an ass of myself. Am trying to raise money to buy a house of my own. Never had my own roof over me. I want a place now—near the Mississippi—near the niggers.

I'll lecture, spit over the top of boxcars, do anything to get it but make love to ladies I do not fancy.

I'll get it some way. Have got to do that before I can think of Paris again but I think often, often of you.

Lots of love.

Sherwood Anderson.

22. Henry McBride was an art critic for the New York Sun.

23. Anderson's words on the jacket of Hemingway's In Our Time (New York: Boni & Liveright, 1925) are: "Mr. Hemingway is young, strong, full of laughter, and he can write. His people flash suddenly up into those odd elusive moments of glowing reality, the clear putting down of which has always made good writing so good."

29

My dear Sherwood,

I was glad to hear from you several people have turned up lately who have seen you in New York and they all told me about you and that was pleasant but it is even pleasanter hearing from you directly. I am sorry in a way that the home on the Mississippi has to be bought before you can come to Paris but I can understand it alright, a home on the Mississippi is better than just a vacation in Paris. One does like the Mississippi. I have just sent you the X Libris with a little thing about your book that I hope you will like and also the announcements of my *Making of Americans* which I am sure you will like. I will send you a copy as soon as it is printed, I am working on the proofs now and I guess it really will be out in September. I have been doing a lot of work beside it has been a pleasant and profitable winter, not too cold and not too warm. I was pleased the other day when one of the new young french group the surrealists told me they liked my valentine on you almost better than anything else of mine, they all can quote the beginning of it which is more than I can do. I hope to have it printed in a volume of *Portraits and Prayers*[24] which looks as if it might get itself published. Haven't seen much of Hemingway this winter he spent most of his time in Austria he is back now with a beard and awfully pleased about his book. Well good luck to you and the Mississippi and do let me hear from you

> Always
> Gtde.

Miss Stein's review of A Story Teller's Story *appeared, with a companion review by Ernest Hemingway, in a publication of the American Library of Paris,* Ex Libris *2 (March 1925): 177.*

24. (New York: Random House, 1934.)

30 A STITCH IN TIME SAVES NINE.
BIRDS OF A FEATHER FLOCK TOGETHER.
CHICKENS COME HOME TO ROOST.

There are four men so far in American letters who have essential intelligence. They are Fenimore Cooper, William Dean Howells, Mark Twain and Sherwood Anderson. They do not reflect life or describe life or embroider life or photograph life, they express life and to express life takes essential intelligence. Whether to express life is the most interesting thing to do or the most important thing to do I do not know, but I do know that it is the most permanent thing to do.

Sherwood Anderson has been doing this thing from his beginning. The development of the quality of this doing has been one of steady development, steady development of his mind and character, steady development in the completion of this expression. The story-teller's story is like all long books uneven but there is no uncertainty in the fullness of its quality. In detail in the beginning and it does begin, in the beginning there is the complete expression of a game, the boys are and they feel they are and they have completely been and they completely are. I think no one can hesitate before the reality of the expression of the life of the Anderson boys. And then later, the living for and by clean linen and the being of the girl who has to have and to give what is needed is without any equal in quality in anything that has been done up to this time by any one writing to-day.

The story-teller's story is not a story of events or experiences it is a story of existence, and the fact that the story teller exists makes a story and keeps on making a story. The story-teller's story will live because the story-teller is alive. As he is alive and as his gift is the complete expression of that life it will continue to live.

31

Dear Gertrude Stein—

I got your fine letter the other day and today got the magazine containing the reviews written by you and Hemingway. I am putting in a note for him. Do not have his address. I wrote a crackerjack review for the jacket of his book and will review it when it comes out. Have already asked one of the bigger reviews to save it for me.[25]

Note also the announcement of your new book. Am crazy to see it.

Have decided to leave Huebsch and am going to Liveright, the same people who are doing the Hemingway book. They made me a generous offer for my books for the next five years and got them.

Have just finished the new novel. I think it is good. Will call it *Dark Laughter* and Liveright will publish it in the fall.[26]

Your review of *Story Teller* was great. I loved it. You always manage to say so much and say it straighter than anyone else I know. Bless you for it.

Guess we'll stay here this summer as we want to get our new house underway. It's going to be fun to fix up a place of our own. If it gets too hot we'll run off to the mountains.

Lots of love.

Sherwood Anderson

25. Anderson apparently did not finally publish any review of *In Our Time*, possibly because he learned of Hemingway's forthcoming literary parody *The Torrents of Spring* (New York: Scribner's, 1926). See Ray Lewis White, "Hemingway's Private Explanation of *The Torrents of Spring*," *Modern Fiction Studies* 13 (Summer 1967): 291–93.

26. *Dark Laughter* appeared on September 15, 1925.

32

[Belley, summer, 1925]

My dear Sherwood,

We are correcting proofs and getting the long book in shape, a quarter of it is already printed and we are going on and on, it is a bit monumental and sometimes seems foolishly youthful now after 20 years but I am leaving it as it is after all it was all done then.[27] There are almost as many dishes and fish to eat here as on the Mississippi and so we prosper greatly, am doing a lot of work too, rather pleased with it—and you, will write soon

Always
Gtde Stein

33

Troutdale, Va.
August 3, 1925.

Gertrude Stein
27 Rue de Fleurus
Paris, France.

My dear Gertrude Stein:

I am immensely excited about your new book and looking forward to seeing it. Boni & Liveright are bringing out a novel of mine this fall. I am calling it *Dark Laughter*. This spring I went to work on a book to be called *A Mid-American Childhood*.[28] I wrote a great deal on it, and threw it away. Now at last it seems to be going.

Elizabeth and I came up here to a little Virginia town two or

27. Miss Stein refers to *The Making of Americans* (Paris: Contact Editions, 1925).
28. Published as *Tar: A Midwest Childhood* (New York: Boni & Liveright, 1926).

three weeks ago and now the book seems to be going alright. We are in a primitive part of old Virginia, near the Tennessee line in a beautiful country, among charming people.

I think I will buy a summer farm here and spend several months each year here in the hills. It is up 3,000 feet and deliciously cool. Not very far from your old home in Baltimore, at least not far compared with the distance from New Orleans.

I am going to do some lecturing this winter and try to make some money, then next fall perhaps we can come to Paris. Give my love to the Hemingways and when you have the proofs of the book out of the way write me a long letter.

With love,
Sherwood Anderson

34

Hotel Pernollet
Belley
Ain
[August, 1925]

My dear Sherwood,

Awfully pleased to hear from you and from Virginia, it is a charming country alright, we used to go to a part of West Va. like that and the people were nice to know, you always make me feel very close to the America I knew but I would like to see you both in Paris one of these days just the same and I hope we will even if you have to lecture. What do you lecture about but I don't suppose you have to lecture about you just lecture and that would be quite nice enough. Anyhow I do want to see you again and so best luck to you for it. Here is the title page and cover of my book. It came to 925 pages and has been a pleasure to do and rather strange to do, you see I have not read it all these years. I did it just after *Three Lives* and I went on and on with it and I finished it, and then it was pretty hopeless and it is only recently thanks to various people among whom Hemingway counts largely as it was he who urged its being at least begun in the Transatlantic[29] that it came up again I am enormously interested in what you will think of it. It has been printed in France and lots of people will think many strange things in it as to tenses and persons and adjectives and adverbs and divisions are due to the french compositors' errors but they are not it is quite as I worked at it and even when I tried to change it well I didn't really try but I went over it to see if it could go different and I always found myself forced back into its incorrectnesses so there they stand. There are some pretty wonderful sentences in it and we know how fond we both are of sentences. As soon as I can get a copy of it from the printer I will send it to you because I do want you to have it more than anybody, well that's all there is of that. Other news this summer I have none. It's a nice part of the country here some day I would like to show it to you we are always talking of building a small thing on a spot we have chosen over the meadows off the Rhône, I have a great weakness for the Rhône valley. In between all this I have been working on three things one of them moderately long one shorter and one shorter still. One is a novel in my fashion and the other is "Phenomena of Nature" also in my fashion, and the third is a "Third."[30] Someday I would like the three together in a book, well some day. Anyway we will be seeing you both before that and always best of luck and feelings to you

Gtde Stein

Address Paris as we will be back in two weeks.

G.S.

29. *The Making of Americans* was serialized in the *Transatlantic Review* 1–2 (April–December 1924).

30. *A Novel of Thank You;* "Natural Phenomena," in *Painted Lace and Other Pieces, 1914–1937*, introduction by Daniel-Henry Kahnweiler (New Haven: Yale University Press, 1955), pp. 167–233; "A Third," in *As Fine as Melanctha*, pp. 329–57.

35

Mrs. Gertrude Stein,
27 Rue de Fleurus,
Paris, France

Dear Gertrude Stein:

I wrote to Boni & Liveright the other day and asked them to send you a copy of the new novel at once. Advance copies are out and they should be able to mail it at once.

I am tremendously anxious to see your own book and hope we may both see you next year.

Now we are back in New Orleans and it is hot. I hope after this year we will never have to spend another summer in the city. I am going to try and buy a small farm over in the Virginia hills and spend the summers there at work. We will have to build us a little house but can build it out of the stones in the creek that goes by the door. I hope we will be doing that next summer and then I hope we can come to Europe in the fall.

I don't lecture about anything in particular except about writing in general. It is silly business but brings in money and money coming in does help a lot.

If we get to Europe next fall we will come in October or November. Both Paris and London ought to be nice then.

I am doing a book on childhood in the Middlewest and am trying to get it into shape so it will be off my hands when I have to go lecturing.

Give my love to the Hemingways. If we come next fall I hope they will be there.

I will be watching every mail for your book.

With love,
Sherwood Anderson

36

My dear Sherwood,

I have kind of been waiting for a letter from you because I do want very much to know how you like my long book but I know you are awfully busy these days and yet I would like to hear. I suppose lecturing is all over and you are back to writing, I guess that is always nicer. I have promised to do a lecture too, I am going to speak to the literary societies of Cambridge and Oxford on my work, I have it all prepared but never having done anything of the kind I feel a bit anxious about the reading of it.[31] Otherwise I have been busy in the usual way, I finished my "Natural Phenomena" and I am now going on with my long novel I don't suppose it will be as long as my long book. They have been lecturing about you here at the Sorbonne and the young crowd are very much interested. They are nice young fellows among them and I think you will like it here when you come. When are you coming—I am going to be in England the beginning of June but I do not suppose you really will come until the fall well anyway write to me and remember me to Mrs Anderson

Always
Gtde Stein

37

Dear Friend—

I am roaming about the country lecturing—getting money to pay for my farm and build a house on it.

31. In May, 1926, Gertrude Stein read "Composition as Explanation" —first at Cambridge University and then at Oxford.

Mrs. A[nderson] came to meet me at Cincinnati and told me your book had come. I'm glad. Wish I were at home. Will write you when I do get there.

At Pittsburgh yesterday heard of a young instructor who almost lost his job because he cares for your books.

My new novel is selling. We are coming to Paris next fall—sure.

Every place I go someone corners me and says—"For God sake explain Gertrude Stein." I grin and back away.

Love to Hemingways,
Sherwood Anderson.

38

New Orleans, La.,
April 25, 1926.

Mlle. Gertrude Stein,
27 Rue de Fleurus
Paris, France.

My dear Gertrude Stein:

I just received your letter in the midst of packing up to go away to the country. We have got a little farm up there and are going there to spend the summer.

Your new book came when I was away lecturing and got put away with a lot of other books and was sent up to the farm with the lot, where it has been resting peacefully ever since. One of the reasons I am so anxious to get up there is that I may dip into the book.

Yesterday I saw a little story of Hemingway's in the Quarter.[32] It was a beautiful story, beautifully done. Lordy but that man can write.

32. "The Undefeated," This Quarter 1 (Autumn–Winter 1925–26): 203–32.

I am having the *Notebook* published this spring.[33] A rather slight thing I think but I am going to send you a copy when it comes.

We have our plans all made for coming to Europe in the fall, perhaps as late as November. I am up to my eyes in a new novel and that, with the mess of getting packed and getting off to the country, has kept me pretty much up in the air. It will be great fun to see you again.

I am going to write you about the book as soon as I get up to the farm and get settled.

With love,
Sherwood

39

Troutdale
Va.
[May 23, 1926]

May 23rd. . .

My files are all packed and your exact address is in them. I shall write you today but may not be able to send this for a week. I had saved your book for the quiet of the country and have been dipping into it. I find the same music I always find in your prose, the thing that always stirs me in everything you write. The music is only more complete, more sustained. I know of no other way to express what I mean. I sent you my *Notebook*. It is a fragmentary thing.

When I got up here I got at once into a new novel. That has absorbed me. I keep your book here on my desk. I steal from it.

My cabin is beautifully located in the half wild hills. I hope to stay here about eight months of the year, the rest of the time in civilization, New York or Europe now and then if I

33. *Sherwood Anderson's Notebook* (New York: Boni & Liveright, 1926).

can afford it. As you know I am hoping for a sight of Paris and you this fall. It depends on how my money holds out.

I have a friend, a young man from California, coming to Europe who wants to meet you and Hemingway. I took the liberty of giving him a note to you. He may not get to Paris before fall.[34]

I can hear the saws and the hammers going. I am getting me a house. It is for me a grand feeling.

Much love
Sherwood Anderson

40

[New Orleans, May 23, 1926]

Miss Gertrude Stein.

I have given this note to you to Mr. Ralph Church. I wrote you about him. I gave him a note to Hemingway but did not have Hemingway's address. Do see that he meets Hemingway and anyone else you think of. He is a very particular friend of mine.

Sincerely.
Sherwood Anderson

41

Gertrude Stein
27 Rue de Fleurus
Paris
[June, 1926]

My dear Sherwood,

It was nice getting a letter from you and that perhaps you will be coming over this fall, I am looking forward to seeing

34. Anderson refers to Ralph Church, who studied at Oxford, came to know Gertrude Stein in Paris, and later taught esthetics at Cornell University.

you. My lecture in Oxford and Cambridge went off very well, it is to be printed by the Hogarth people under the title, *Composition as an Explanation*,[35] I think you will like it. They have not sent me the *Note-book* and I do want very much to have it,

Always
Gtde Stein.

42

Sherwood Anderson
Ripshin Farm
P. O. Grant. Virginia
July 15, 1926

Gertrude Stein
27 Rue de Fleurus
Paris, France

Dear Gertrude Stein:

I got your note and will send you a copy of the *Notebook* from here so that I will not have to depend on the publisher. I wish I might have heard you lecture in Oxford and Cambridge. I sent off my *Childhood* book to the publisher the other day and am deep in the new novel.

We are having great fun building a stone house on the farm and still planning to be in Paris sometime next winter.

With Love
Sherwood Anderson

35. Leonard and Virginia Woolf published *Composition as Explanation* in London at the Hogarth Press in 1926.

43

Hotel Pernollet
Belley
Ain
[August, 1926]

My dear Sherwood,

The *Note-book* came and I have enjoyed it immensely particularly Stieglitz and the New Orleans David,[36] you know some day Sherwood you must write a novel that is just one portrait you are a peach of a portraitist do sometime do a novel that is just one portrait and nobody else's feelings coming in, I can't tell you how I am looking forward to seeing you in Paris, you will be sure to come, my Oxford Cambridge lecture is coming out in the November number of the *Dial*[37] I am very pleased with that and I hope you will be too, best to you and Mrs Anderson and surely this winter

Always
Gtde Stein

44

Ripshin Farm
Grant, Virginia
Aug. 26, 1926

Gertrude Stein
27 Rue de Fleurus.
Paris, France

Dear Gertrude Stein:

I had your nice note from Belley but thought I had better send this letter to your Paris address. I shall look forward to

36. "Alfred Stieglitz," pp. 149–59; "David" is actually William Faulkner in "A Meeting South," pp. 101–21.
37. "Composition as Explanation," *Dial* 71 (October 1926): 327–36.

seeing the Oxford lecture in the *Dial*. I am delighted of course that you like the *Notebook* and hope you will like the child story that is to be published this fall.

Just now I am having a great time building a house on the farm but just the same I am scribbling away every spare moment.

It will be fun to see you and talk with you again.

Sherwood Anderson

In the first week of December, 1926, Sherwood Anderson sailed for Europe on the S.S. Roosevelt. His second trip to Europe, which lasted until March 4, 1927, was much less happy than the 1921 tour had been, perhaps because Anderson took with him his third wife, Elizabeth Prall Anderson, and John and Marion, two children from his unhappy first marriage.

45

[Paris, December, 1926]

Dear Gertrude Stein

We got in from London last night.

I was so happy to be in Paris—after London. I drank too much. This morning my hands shake but I am still happy to be here.

Nothing would keep us from the Christmas Eve party. Mr. Church cannot come as he is going for Christmas to his mother at Aix.

I shall give myself the pleasure of coming to call on you very soon.

Sincerely
Sherwood Anderson

46

[Paris, December, 1926]

Dear Gertrude

Have been laid up again but am better.

Will you and Miss Toklas go with us to the Jolas apartment Thursday evening?[38] We would come for you about 8:30.

Maria sings some marvelous negro songs I want you to hear.

With love
Sherwood

47

[Paris, December, 1926]

Dear Gertrude

Surely it will be o.k. to bring Virgil Thomson. Elliot Paul will be there.[39] We will come for you about 8:30.

When you know my fool illnesses you cannot possibly take them seriously.

It will be good to see you.

Sherwood

48

[Paris, January, 1927]

Dear Gertrude Stein.

Church can be addressed at Oriel College, Oxford. I haven't his residence address but a note to the college will get him.

---

38. Eugène Jolas, born in the United States of a French father and a German mother, had met Sherwood Anderson in New Orleans and had afterward moved to France. Anderson had written the "Introduction" to Jolas's English poems, *Cinema* (New York: Adelphi Company, 1926).

39. The American composer Virgil Thomson (1896–) lived in Paris from 1925 to 1940 and met Gertrude Stein in the autumn of 1926. Elliot Paul (1891–1958), expatriate American journalist who in 1927 founded and edited the magazine *transition*.

He will be delighted, I'm sure, to meet anyone you may send to him.

Will try to get in to Miss Barney[40] Friday but am not sure.

By the way Mr. Church's mother is here and we would like to bring her in some evening.

As Always
Sherwood Anderson

49

My Dear Gertrude Stein—

We will be delighted to come Sunday at 12:30.

We dropped in to see you last Sunday evening but were unlucky enough to find you out.

Sincerely
Sherwood Anderson

50

[Paris, February, 1927]

Dear Miss Stein—

If it is OK with you I will bring Miss Henderson of New Orleans in to see you next Tuesday evening.

This is the woman about whom I spoke to you at Miss Barney's.

Sincerely
Sherwood Anderson

---

40. Natalie Clifford Barney, one of Gertrude Stein's American friends in Paris, conducted something of a literary *salon* for "international" authors.

51

Dear Gertrude

This is just a note to say that John is about again and will be very glad to come with us on Wednesday.

We look forward to seeing you both with delight.

With Love
Sherwood

Just as Anderson had recorded in a diary his impressions of Gertrude Stein in 1921, he wrote of her briefly in a 1926–27 diary of his days in Europe. The brief entry, now nearly illegible, follows Anderson's musing on the role of Americans in Paris and ends in obscurity.

52

I go to see G[ertrude] Stein because I think that in any event she will be [the] same.

She is.

Having stirred her into doing it she also speaks of America & in particular of New York. It is her notion that we in America have made our greatest mistake in not having had our seat of government there.

"Life in New York should be more ceremonial," she says. "My God," I say to myself, "is she a royalist too?" She disclaims anything of the great. "The greatest city should be the seat of government," she says but declares herself a firm republican.

She only wants more trapping to republican life. U.S. senators wearing golden robes perhaps. The president sweeping down Fifth Ave. on a white charger or in a snow white automobile. Great capitol building towering above the sky scrapers of New York. The government, not the city, asserting itself to the world.

"There is something missing," she says. New York should at least be to America what R[ome] is to Italy, Paris to Russia, [?Greece] to Germany, London to Paris.

53

Hamburg-Amerika Line
On the boat
[March, 1927]

Dear Gertrude

A very very German boat. It is slow. We go to Halifax, then Boston, then New York. All of which we did not know when we got on. They concealed the facts admirably.

The weather cold and grey. Elizabeth was seasick but now walks about. We hear German, read books, drink beer. The Germans may have suffered some lack of food during the war. They may be preparing for another war. Every time you turn your head there is a man with a tray of food. The call to the dining room sounds constantly.

I seem destined not to be excited by the Germans or English. In an odd way the French seem closer to me.

What shall I say to you and Miss Toklas that will a little express my gratitude to you? I shall not try. It is an impossible task. For five years—since I saw you both the last time—I have been seeing that great sweet room of yours in every detail. Now I shall see it as rearranged. Do not rearrange it again until I come again.

I love you both—the place where you live—the spirit of your house.

I have a sort of feeling that you, Gertrude, may be coming more fully into recognition. I may be wrong. It isn't so terribly important to you—I dare say.

A queer six months of pause for me. Anyway I have feelers out. If I had you to talk with more often it would be a great help.

In the summer Elizabeth's brother David will come to Paris. I hope he can see you. He will be much with Church as they are great friends. I'll depend on Church to bring him.

Write us now and then—at Grant, Va.

We may do the Grant[41] thing together yet.

When I am more in form.

With Love
Sherwood.

54

Hotel Pernollet
Belley
Ain
[Summer, 1927]

My dear Sherwood,

How goes it, here we are in the country and liking it and wishing we might show you and Elizabeth some of it but some year we will. We are still parlying about our little house up here it takes an everlasting lot of parlying but we get a little nearer all the time and one of these days we will surprise ourselves by having it. Nothing very different in Paris after you left xcept that you were not there. We saw John quite frequently and had news of you in that way, we got very attached to him, at times he is an awful lot like you and then Church turned up and we saw him just before leaving. His eyes are much better and he is as nice as ever. I worked a lot this spring

---

41. Both Sherwood Anderson and Gertrude Stein were fascinated by Ulysses S. Grant, although their much-discussed "collaboration" never was written. In 1931 Miss Stein wrote "Grant," in *Four In America*, introduction by Thornton Wilder (New Haven: Yale University Press, 1947), pp. 3–81.

a lot and a lot and have been kind of laying off latterly but the pot is beginning to simmer but I am putting off the boiling as long as possible. And what are you doing do tell me and all about yourselves and lots of love

Always
Gtde.

55

Ripshin Farm
Grant, Virginia
[Summer, 1927]

Dear Friend—

Every day I have been thinking of you, of Miss Alice and your house.

Why have I not written?

I always feel writing letters is more or less senseless—to you. Surely I love you always.

We are in the country. It is beautiful here. The pear, apple, plum and cherry trees blossom madly.

I play the phonograph, I walk, I scribble some.

The birds sing. Something inside me—like a black still pool that has not stirred for a long time—is stirring. What will pop up out of it I do not know.

You were infinitely good for me this winter. Bless you and your house.

Elizabeth is well, is making garden and sends love.

Sherwood

56

[Troutdale, fall, 1927]

Dear Gertrude. . .

A dumb summer after a dumb winter. Have been in a continuous jam. Now I think I am getting out. Made up my mind that the grand trouble with me was that I was trying to live by writing. It is so easy over here and so difficult. I had begun trying to work on a schedule and was pressing, off my stroke, etc. Up until two or three years ago, as I guess you know, I had always made my living by writing advertisements. Hated to go back to that but had made up my mind to do it.

Then something came up. Near me is a county town named Marion, Virginia. It is a prosperous little town, county seat, etc., and has a weekly paper that makes money. It is filled with town news, who married, who went to visit Aunt Mary, who died, etc., etc. The man who owned it had to sell and I am buying it and hope to live by it.

That is my definite news. I did not want to write anything that was not fun doing. I knew that if I went on trying to make my living by it I would soon be a hack. I shall not try to do anything with the paper—I mean in the way of uplifting the town. I'll just run around and get the local news and stick it in. Have an idea it will be great fun.

Aside from that there is no news. We are in the country. It is gorgeous here now. Most of the year I can drive to my newspaper over the mountains. When the snow is deep I shall have to stay over there about four days a week.

Of course I am on a book but I am going to let it take its own time. Write me news of yourself.

Sherwood A[nderson]

My love to Miss Alice, Elizabeth sends love to you both.

57

[Marion, spring, 1928]

Dear Gertrude—

Been sitting all day in the court room hearing a murder trial, and half sick that nothing I write seems as vital—

Then running across an alleyway to my little shop.

I surely will send a paper and now. We are just getting one out.

The town band is practising. It is night. The town is full of people.

I am sent for to sheep shearings, cattle judgings—to see apple trees' blossoms. Whatever happens my phone rings. "Come out here and see this or that." Mostly I go.

Such things people believe—and don't believe—about family honor, etc. You should hear a murder trial. Such muddled minds and impulses too.

Wish to God I could see you.

Lots of love from both of us,

Sherwood

58

The Marion Publishing Company
Marion, Virginia
July 31st, 1928.

Gertrude Stein
Hotel Pernollet
Belley, France.

Dear Gertrude:—

We are still here in this little town. Our farm is twenty miles away over the hills. John and Miss Marion are on the farm this summer and we go there for the weekends.

All the work I am doing is the paper, it is a busy and amusing life.

I do not write much. Many projects are in my head but few of them come to anything. It is pleasant to sit thinking of your house in Paris and of you two women there. I wish I had news for you of some great project, but I haven't.

Lots of love to you both,

Sherwood

59

27 Rue de Fleurus
[Winter, 1928]

My dear Sherwood,

Pleasant days to you both and many of them, we always think about you about now because it was so nice having you here two years ago and it would be awfully nice having you here again. What is happening to you these days and how are you liking it. I have heard nothing about you for a long time, I usually have news of you through Ralph Church but he has been doing less of Oxford in Paris than he did, I am xpecting to see him next week though and perhaps he will have heard from you. Anyway do write me a line and tell me about yourself. As for me it is as usual. I am interested enormously just at present in sentences and grammar and verbs and nouns and sometimes in an opera, I have done two operas that would amuse you I think, perhaps some day I can show them to you anyway lots of love to you and to Elizabeth and the best of wishes

Gtde.

60

General Francis Marion Hotel
Marion, Va.
[Winter, 1928]

Dear Friend—

I've been a dog not to write. We are sending you a copy of the paper. It's been the greatest sport I ever got into. I was afraid I couldn't write for our old farmers but they adore it. My circulation is walking right up.

It's a county seat town, court house and jail right by my shop—mountains all around—rich valleys.

Moonshiners in the hills, cattle and sheep raising. I went

over one night recently and sat up with a farmer and his sheep
—the lambing going on.

I don't write letters much—I can't with lambs being born
and bootleggers being tried and plowing, seeding and fishing.
I've always had too much energy to just be a writer. If I can't
write incidentally—as I go—I'll let it go.

The papers keep me eternally busy. I practically write them
all, get in the news, write advertisements.

Do give my love to Miss Alice, Church and others—whom-
ever you see I know.

Have you met David Prall—Elizabeth's brother? You'll like
him.

Sherwood.

61

The Marion Publishing Company
Marion, Virginia
January 15, 1929.

Gertrude Stein
27 Rue de Fleurus
Paris, France.

Dear Gertrude Stein:—

I am ashamed that I have not written you any letters for a
long time.

Everything of my routine of life has been disturbed for a
long time now. I have been trying to work, but have not got
much done. It has been very interesting and absorbing running
the country weeklies during the last year—but they have taken
a lot of time.

Now my son, Bob, who is twenty-one, is with me and will be
able to do a lot of the work. I hope to be able to get free from
so many of the details that had piled up on me and that I shall
have a book or two in the next year.

I think often of you in Paris and your house.

I think anyone who at all follows writing sees also your influence everywhere.

With lots of love and luck to you and your house.

                                                    Sherwood.

62

27 Rue de Fleurus
[February, 1929]

My dear Sherwood,

Awfully glad to hear from you but disappointed that there is nothing said about your coming over. Ralph Church held out the hope that you were going to lecture in Sweden and we all xpected that you would stop over coming or going and it would have been nice seeing you, it's about time we were meeting again I liked it, anyhow I am glad that you are going to have another book or so, they take a lot of interest in you here, and down in the country in Belley, where we are getting to know a lot of the people they are all awfully interested in your work. Everything is peaceful with us, we have at last gotten our country house we told you about and it would be nice seeing you there and showing you a little french country life, I am working fairly steadily on the sentence, I am making a desperate effort to find out what is and isn't a sentence, having been brought up in a good old public school grammar and sentences are a fascinating subject to me. I struggled all last year with grammar, vocabulary is easier, and now I think before more grammar I must find out what is the essence of a sentence, sometimes I almost know but not yet quite, I think it will interest you, otherwise we have been busy with a translation of 60 pages of *Making of Americans*, it was rather interesting particularly as my young translator knows no English,[42] well anyway it would be nice seeing you most awfully nice, are you going to Sweden and do give my love to Elizabeth and lots to yourself

Always
Gtde.

63

[Marion, Virginia]
April 2, 1929.

Gertrude Stein:—

I am writing this letter for my dear friends, Mr. and Mrs. Burton Emmett of New York.[43] They are coming to Paris early in May [and] both Mr. & Mrs. Emmett are interested in painting and painters and Mr. Emmett is a collector of fine prints.

Both Mr. and Mrs. Emmett have been very kind to me and you would do me a great favor by having them to call on you to let them see your paintings and yourself.

If Ralph Church is in town ask him to meet Mr. Emmett and tell him some of the interesting old places to go to in Paris, if Church is still in England perhaps some other young man among your acquaintances will do this nice thing for me and my friends.

Sincerely,
[Sherwood Anderson]

---

42. Perhaps "La Fabrication des Américains," a translation by Gertrude Stein and Georges Hugnet now in Yale University's archive of Stein manuscripts.

43. Burton Emmett, a very rich advertising executive, had financed Anderson's country newspaper career in Marion, Virginia, in exchange for most of Anderson's literary manuscripts. Apparently the Emmetts did not meet Gertrude Stein in France until 1933.

64

The Marion Publishing Company
Marion, Virginia
[Summer, 1929]

Dear Friend

I am asking Mrs. Cornelia Anderson, John and Marion's mother, to come and call on you while she is in Paris this summer.

I hope she may be lucky enough to find you in town.

With love
Sherwood Anderson

65

[Florida, January, 1930]

Dear Gertrude Stein,

Your note came to me far down South on Tampa Bay. I've been down here several weeks, drifting about. My son Bob is, in the meantime, running the newspapers in Virginia. I really don't know how long I shall stay just here but intend to spend the winter floating about the south. I love it.

I am on several things but none of them have fruitioned in a way to make me very proud of them.

Wish I could drop in on you for a chat but you are so far away.

Lots of love just the same.

Sherwood Anderson.

66

Plain Edition
27 Rue de Fleurus (VI)
Paris [early 1930]

My dear Sherwood,

Ralph Church was just here and he says you are back in Marion and seem to be enjoying yourself both as a poet and a man of action, well we too, as you will see by the enclosed action is it, I just got tired of shoving others so we decided to shove ourselves for a change,[44] and I think perhaps it is a good thing, anyway I hope you like its looks, no Paris in yours and no Marion in ours and yet it would be most awfully nice to meet in fact I don't know of anything that would be nicer, I suppose Ralph keeps you informed of all the Paris news, there always is a good deal but it goes on and it changes so fast there is not much to tell but there always is lots of affection for you

In me
Gtde.

67

[Georgia]
Sunday, April 19 [1930]

Dear Gertrude Stein

Your letter reached me at a lumber camp back in the Georgia hills. I have been here for some weeks, trout fishing and trying to put into prose the impressions of the winter.

I have rather gone in for American industry and have been spending most of the winter inside factories—trying to get into prose some feeling of modern machinery.

44. Gertrude Stein refers to the above letterhead, which announces the "Plain Edition," a series of Miss Stein's works published by Alice Toklas.

It has at least been exciting. I have got a few things, some of which seem to me to approach true poetry.

I think I'll keep at it.

Lots of love,
Sherwood Anderson

On August 31, 1933, Gertrude Stein published her most popular book, confusing almost no one with the title The Autobiography of Alice B. Toklas. *The following passages on Sherwood Anderson, showing Miss Stein's sincere appreciation of Anderson's first visit with her in 1921 and their mutual dislike of Ernest Hemingway after 1926, are reprinted from the* Autobiography *(New York: Harcourt, Brace, 1933), pp. 241–42, 265–66, 268, 302–4.*

68 FROM *The Autobiography of Alice B. Toklas*

Sylvia Beach from time to time brought groups of people to the house, groups of young writers and some older women with them. It was at that time that Ezra Pound came, no that was brought about in another way. She later ceased coming to the house but she sent word that Sherwood Anderson had come to Paris and wanted to see Gertrude Stein and might he come. Gertrude Stein sent back word that she would be very pleased and he came with his wife and Rosenfeld, the musical critic.

For some reason or other I was not present on this occasion, some domestic complication in all probability, at any rate when I did come home Gertrude Stein was moved and pleased as she has very rarely been. Gertrude Stein was in those days a little bitter, all her unpublished manuscripts, and no hope of publication or serious recognition. Sherwood Anderson came and quite simply and directly as is his way told her what he thought of her work and what it had meant to him in his development. He told it to her then and what was even rarer he told it in print immediately after. Gertrude Stein and Sherwood Anderson have always been the best of friends but I do not believe even he realises how much his visit meant to her. It was he who thereupon wrote the introduction to Geography and Plays. . . .

Gertrude Stein and Sherwood Anderson are very funny on the subject of Hemingway. The last time that Sherwood was in Paris they often talked about him. Hemingway had been formed by the two of them and they were both a little proud and a little ashamed of the work of their minds. Hemingway had at one moment, when he had repudiated Sherwood Anderson and all his works, written him a letter in the name of american literature which he, Hemingway, in company with his contemporaries was about to save, telling Sherwood just what he, Hemingway thought about Sherwood's work, and, that thinking, was in no sense complimentary. When Sherwood came to Paris Hemingway naturally was afraid. Sherwood as naturally was not.

As I say he and Gertrude Stein were endlessly amusing on the subject. They admitted that Hemingway was yellow, he is, Gertrude Stein insisted, just like the flat-boat men on the Mississippi river as described by Mark Twain. But what a book, they both agreed, would be the real story of Hemingway, not those he writes but the confessions of the real Ernest Hemingway. It would be for another audience than the audience Hemingway now has but it would be very wonderful. And then they both agreed that they have a weakness for Hemingway because he is such a good pupil. He is a rotten pupil, I protested. You don't understand, they both said, it is so flattering to have a pupil who does it without understanding it, in other words he takes training and anybody who takes training is a favourite pupil. They both admit it to be a weakness. Gertrude Stein added further, you see he is like Derain. You remember Monsieur de Tuille said, when I did not understand why Derain was having the success he was having that it was because he looks like a modern and he smells of the museums. And that is Hemingway, he looks like a modern and he smells of the museums. But what a story that of the real Hem, and one he should tell himself but alas he never will. After all, as he himself once murmured, there is the career, the career. . . .

In those early days Hemingway liked all his contemporaries except Cummings. He accused Cummings of having copied everything, not from anybody but from somebody. Gertrude Stein who had been much impressed by The Enormous Room said that Cummings did not copy, he was the natural heir of the New England tradition with its aridity and its sterility, but also with its individuality. They disagreed about this. They also disagreed about Sherwood Anderson. Gertrude Stein contended that Sherwood Anderson had a genius for using the sentence to convey a direct emotion, this was in the great american tradition, and that really except Sherwood there was no one in America who could write a clear and passionate sentence. Hemingway did not believe this, he did not like Sherwood's taste. Taste has nothing to do with sentences, contended Gertrude Stein. She also added that Fitzgerald was the only one of the younger writers who wrote naturally in sentences. . . .

Sherwood came to Paris that winter and he was a delight. He was enjoying himself and we enjoyed him. He was being lionised and I must say he was a very appearing and disappearing lion. I remember his being asked to the Pen Club. Natalie Barney and a long-bearded frenchman were to be his sponsors. He wanted Gertrude Stein to come too. She said she loved him very much but not the Pen Club. Natalie Barney came over to ask her. Gertrude Stein who was caught outside, walking her dog, pleaded illness. The next day Sherwood turned up. How was it, asked Gertrude Stein. Why, said he, it wasn't a party for me, it was a party for a big woman, and she was just a derailed freight car.

We had installed electric radiators in the studio, we were as our finnish servant would say getting modern. She finds it difficult to understand why we are not more modern. Gertrude Stein says that if you are way ahead with your head you naturally are old fashioned and regular in your daily life. And Picasso adds, do you suppose Michael Angelo would have been grateful for a gift of a piece of renaissance furniture, no he wanted a greek coin.

We did install electric radiators and Sherwood turned up and we gave him a Christmas party. The radiators smelled and it was terrifically hot but we were all pleased as it was a nice party. Sherwood looked as usual very handsome in one of his very latest scarf ties. Sherwood Anderson does dress well and his son John follows suit. John and his sister came over with their father. While Sherwood was still in Paris John the son was an awkward shy boy. The day after Sherwood left John turned up, sat easily on the arm of the sofa and was beautiful to look upon and he knew it. Nothing to the outward eye had changed but he had changed and he knew it.

It was during this visit that Gertrude Stein and Sherwood Anderson had all those amusing conversations about Hemingway. They enjoyed each other thoroughly. They found out that they both had had and continued to have Grant as their great american hero. They did not care so much about Lincoln either of them. They had always and still liked Grant. They even planned collaborating on a life of Grant. Gertrude Stein still likes to think about this possibility.

69

Dear Gertrude Stein—

I have been reading with joy the autobiography as it came along in the magazine—a bit sorry and sad on the night after that number when you took such big patches of skin off Hemmy with your delicately held knife—[45]

But great joy in the whole performance.

I wrote one good story last winter—in a book called *Death in the Woods*—I'd send the book on to you only the publisher went smash and I haven't any copies.[46] The story I liked best was called "Brother Death."

I made a play out of the *Winesburg* stories—the Theatre Guild theatre to do.

Now I am in a long thing that promises to be fun.

I am in the country—on my farm in the hills of Virginia. Why don't you and Alice come to America—as a great adventure, next summer—Ford around, come see us and others?

And there is something else. There is such a fat juicy taste to your book. Do another all about people seen and felt—as you see and feel them—all kinds of people—their talks—your talks with them—impressions—well you'll know.

You ought now to have one big taste—square meal—of America again, don't you think?

Sherwood

---

45. Four sections of *The Autobiography of Alice B. Toklas* were published in the *Atlantic Monthly* from May through August, 1933. Anderson refers to "Ernest Hemingway and the Post-War Decade. . . ," 152 (August 1933): 197–208.
46. *Death in the Woods and Other Stories* (New York: Liveright, Inc., 1933).

70

Dear Gertrude Stein

I have taken the liberty of asking two friends—Burt and Mary Emmett—to come call on you. They are old friends and have been extraordinarily kind to me. I am in fact, at this moment, living in their house—54 Washington Mews in New York—they having given me the use of the house for the winter.

Besides all this they are very sweet people.

Lots of love to both of you.

Sherwood Anderson

71

Bilignin par Belley
Ain
[November, 1933]

My dearest Sherwood

It has been nice hearing from you and I hope you liked the whole book once you had it, it will be very nice seeing the Emmetts but a whole lot [nicer] to hear all about you, we are still in the country, the country is such an active place, I understand what the french mean when they say that they have to go to a big city to rest, I have never known so many things happen as happen in the country and it would be nice to tell you about them all and to hear all about yours, are you coming over, they all tell me I am going over and perhaps I am, many many years ago when I was young and foolish I said I would only go back to America after I was a real lion, and now I don't know, in any case I do want to see you and hear you. I had a charming letter from an unknown who said she had first learned how to write from reading *Winesburg, Ohio*, and that she had then always read you but never written to you but now she wrote to me, it was rather sweet, lots and lots of love

Gtde.

72

56 Washington Mews
New York, N. Y.
November 18, 1933

Miss Gertrude Stein
27 Rue de Fleurus
Paris, France

My dear Gertrude:

I have had your nice letter on my desk for several days. Some time ago I wrote you about some friends of mine that are in Paris this winter. I hope they come to see you as I think you will like them.

I am sure you know that your book has made a great stir in this country and is being talked about everywhere. It must be fun for you.

I am in New York this winter, staying in a house given me for the winter by Mr. and Mrs. Burton Emmett—old friends of mine—in fact the same friends who are now in Paris and about whom I wrote you. This winter I have been working day and night getting a play ready to go into production, and I think we may get it produced this winter.

I do think it would be great fun if you would decide to come to America next summer. Why don't you? It would be such a joy to all of us.

Give my best to Miss Toklas.

With love,
Sherwood

[78]

73

27 Rue de Fleurus
Paris. [January, 1934]

My dear Sherwood

We were so pleased to have your articles that the Emmetts gave us, I liked the one about Roosevelt immensely and so did Bernard Faÿ and he wants to translate for the french papers and we enjoyed all about you.[47] It would be nice to see and hear you nicer than I can say, you seem in awfully good form and we always like each other a lot. Everything is going on but what else can it do. Anyway I am awfully glad you are going on, and lots of love

Gtde.

74

Marion, Virginia.
January 30, 1934.

Miss Gertrude Stein
27 Rue de Fleurus
Paris, France

Dear Gertrude Stein:

I am enclosing a letter from Helen M. Edwards of Alabama that came to me through an old acquaintance in Washington, Mr. W. R. H. Crump. I have written Helen Edwards telling her that I had no doubt you would see her when she was in Paris, and I want to take advantage of this chance to thank you for being so nice to my New York friends, Mr. and Mrs. Burt Emmett.

47. Probably Anderson's article "Explain! Explain! Again Explain," *Today* 1 (December 2, 1933): 3; Bernard Faÿ, French university professor who translated many of Anderson's writings.

I had a letter from the Emmetts telling me of the delight they had in meeting you and how nice you were to them.

I promised to write about you for the *American Spectator*, and expect to get at the article today after I have completed my dictation. I approach the job with a good deal of hesitancy, and hope I shall have something real to say.

Just at present I have left New York and am running around in the back country doing some articles on people in the back country for a New York magazine. At any rate it is lots of fun and whether the articles are good or bad, I am having a good time at it.

Give my best to Toklas and lots of love to you.

Sincerely,
Sherwood Anderson

In "Has Gertrude Stein a Secret?" Atlantic Monthly, January 1934, pp. 50–57, the psychologist B. F. Skinner attacked Gertrude Stein's writing as deceptively "automatic." Skinner wrote that, as Miss Stein's purpose was not to reveal a second personality through her "automatic writing," her work therefore had nothing valid to say. Sherwood Anderson answered this argument as best he could in "Gertrude Stein," American Spectator 2 (April 1934): 3.

75 GERTRUDE STEIN

An article about Gertrude Stein, by B. F. Skinner, appeared in the January *Atlantic*. Hers is automatic writing. That was the conclusion. A pretty good case was made for the conclusion, but if you think the same result can be accomplished by anyone trying automatic writing, try it. If you happen to be a person of real talent, with a feeling for words, word relationships, word color, you may get something that will surprise and please you. Otherwise you will get pure drivel. It comes to the same thing with all writing—all write as well as they can—what is there comes out.

Color sense is something you must be born with. The painter seeks color and, as any good painter knows, there is form in color. A half hour with nature will prove it to you. Go to a hilltop on any day when the light is waning. There is a valley spread out before you. As the light changes, forms also change. The form of the Spring hill covered with trees is not the same as the form of the same hill, the trees splashed with color in the Fall.

Go into the woods now and begin picking up tiny bits of color. There are broken bits of tree bark, tiny stones, pieces of leaf. Hold these in your cupped hand. Let the light in slowly. See how amazingly the forms change as the light changes the color.

This matter of writing, the use of words in writing, is an odd affair. How much Miss Stein has taught all of us. Let's admit, at the beginning, that there is a confusion here. Words are used to convey thought, but there is for the proseman, as for the poet, such a thing as pure and beautiful prose. At least this may be said for the arts of painting and music: the layman approaches these arts with a humbleness not in him when he approaches prose writing. We prosemen have both the handicap and glory of using man's speech as tools, and I have often heard sentences on the street that glow like jewels. There are critics, in this country, and I presume in all countries, who spend their lives writing about writing and who can never, by any chance, know anything about it. You can't be blamed if you are born color-blind.

When it comes to that, the same thing can be said about a good many writers.

Musicians and painters often have this attitude toward writing and in particular toward prosemen. A man like Hemingway writes a sentence. The man can make sentences. He is one of the few American writers who can.

To be sure, there is something else to writing. Writers also deal with thoughts, impulses in themselves, and other men. It is possible to have a very fine mind, fine impulses, great earnestness, profoundly affect a civilization even, while writing miserably.

A musician, a composer, walking with me, spoke of his art and of my own. He said he envied me. We were standing on a bridge. "There is water flowing under the bridge," he said. "How very simple. You want your reader to know about the water. You say, 'The water runs under the bridge.' There you are."

It is simple, isn't it? A good many books are written in that spirit. As though we writers did not work always for the unnameable overtone—to be got by word color if you please. A few so-called great writers have written without ever touching it. Melville had it, and Borrow—Turgenev superlatively. These are your great writers—writer's writers. They would all have appreciated what Stein has been doing.

This nonsense about automatic writing. All good writing is, in a sense, automatic. It is and it isn't. When I am really writing, not doing as I am doing now, thinking the words out as I go, making an argument, but am really writing, it is always half automatic. There is something stored within that flows out. When you drive an automobile you are not necessarily, at the moment, thinking automobile.

As I write, I am outside the world of reality. Here is a confusion many minds seem unable to get past. The world of art, of any art, is never the real world. The world of the novel, of the story, is not the world of reality. There is a world outside of reality being created. The object is not to be true to the world of reality but to the world outside reality. You want color—word color—that brings vitality also into that world.

In this world, when it is successfully created, everything counts. Word is laid against word as carefully and always instinctively as any painter would lay one color against another.

[82]

Have you got it? You have or you haven't. Thinking, conscious-ness, will not do it. To a good many people all I am saying here will be nonsense. You have been told that Rembrandt was a great painter. Do you know why? A painter should know. You may say what you please to me about the personal character of Mr. George Moore. You may like the man, his mind or his character, or you may not, but if you tell me he was not a very great writer, in a way, for example, that a thousand Thomas Hardys could never be, then I am sure you know nothing of writing.

Stein is great because she is a releaser of talent. She is a path-finder. She has been a great, a tremendous influence among writers because she has dared, in the face of ridicule and mis-understanding, to try to awaken in all of us who write a new feeling for words. She has done it.

"Take the word outside so-called 'sense' for the time if you please," she has said. "Let the word-man in you come forth, dance for a time." For example, it is true of me, as I know it must be of any man who loves writing, that I have at times great difficulty in making the escape out of reality, so-called, into what is the great reality.

It is necessary for the writer to go out and come in by the path of words. The word sense has to be brought back. Color lies in the word, form in the color. There have been ages when all painting was dull and drab. Whistler was a bad painter. He had no color. If you please, he had too much mind, or what he thought was mind. It took a Cézanne to bring color back. "Oh," they cried, "but he has no form. He cannot draw, etc." Hang the Cézanne in your room. The form will come into it. Go from the painting of Madame Cézanne to Whistler's Mother. Now see where the form is, where the drawing.

"The trouble with Stein is that she doesn't make sense."

"Whose sense?"

Wait. Stein is a revolutionist. If we ever get again a world that knows what pure writing is, the sense and form in Stein's work will come through. She also will stand as a restorer of "the word."

76

56 Washington Mews,
New York City.
March 24, 1934.

Miss Gertrude Stein,
27 Rue de Fleurus,
Paris, France.

My dear Gertrude:

I just got back to New York, after my long cruise in the South, and find the town full of talk about the opera.[48] I had the bum luck of being away all the time it was on but Eleanor and her mother went and were tremendously excited by it. I understand it is the whole talk of the season here and that already there is talk of reviving it. I hope this talk may turn out to be true.

I keep getting notes from Burt and Mary Emmett telling me how much joy they have had in meeting you and coming to your house. I think we ought all get together and persuade you now to come over here on a visit. It would be gorgeous if you could do it this summer. Why don't you come to New York, take your bow here, then come down to us in the country? I am pretty sure you would love our hills and mountain people.

It is a grand satisfaction to see everything coming your way after all these years.

Lots of love.

Sincerely,
Sherwood.

Have just heard that the opera is to be revived.

48. On February 20, 1934, Gertrude Stein's "opera" with Virgil Thomson, *Four Saints in Three Acts*, opened in New York City.

77

My dear Sherwood,

Your thing in the *Spectator* pleased and touched me more than anything xcept the first thing you ever wrote about me. I can't tell you how much you always mean to me. This is a beautiful piece of writing. The water does flow under the bridge when you say it does. I am tremendously interested in the whole article. I am and have been very full of meditations about direct and indirect vision, and the relation between the writer and an audience either actual or not actual, I have just been writing about four Americans and one of them Henry James has cleared up a lot of things for me that is in trying to put him down.[49] There are so many things to say and there is nothing to do but say them. And perhaps we will see each other over there. That would be wonderfully nice. We are always very close to each other, and there is so much I want to tell you about what has happened. Well anyway Sherwood they won't say any more about automatism. You have settled all that completely. And wonderfully, I do want very much to see Virginia and you,

> Always
> Gtde.

Gertrude Stein finally agreed to a lecture tour of the United States—her first visit to America since 1904. She landed in New York on October 24, 1934; and her tour was quite successful, for Gertrude Stein had become famous for the alleged obscurity of her works. And she managed to meet her old friend Sherwood Anderson twice—in Minnesota and in New Orleans. Anderson and his wife Eleanor, whom he had married in 1933, tried to see Miss Stein several other times; but their

49. Published as "Henry James," in *Four In America*, pp. 119–59.

schedules could not allow other meetings. Never again would Anderson and Stein be able to meet and talk.

78

Hotel Chelsea
New York
[October, 1934]

Dear Gertrude Stein

I'm upset that I am leaving New York just as you come. On account of some affairs I must go to Virginia today.

Then I am going to the Middlewest. Are you to be out there —Chicago or anywhere?

When and where?

Do drop me a line at:

Marion, Va.

If I am not there it will be sent forward to me.

You will have a grand time.

Love to both of you.

Sherwood A[nderson]

79

Hotel Algonquin
New York
[November 22, 1934]

My dear Sherwood

Yes I am going to be in Chicago and I do most awfully want to see you and it would be nice seeing you down in Va. we are going to be around Richmond Va. in January is that anywhere near you, will you let me hear at the Drake hotel where you are to be, there is no one whom I would rather see but you know that, I am liking everything that is happening an awful lot

Always
Gtde Stein

80

Hotel Elkhart
Elkhart, Indiana
[December, 1934]

Dear Gertrude Stein

I am writing you care of Carl[50] because I do not know how else to reach you. I am out, drifting about in a car in the middle-west. This came about because I had a commission from a magazine to do some articles and terribly needed the money.

I had thought that I would catch up with you in Chicago and say hello to you, greet you, but, by a morning paper I see that you have given up going to Chicago. Is this true and what are your plans? How long will you stay in America, etc.?

I do hope you will stay until summer. I want you to come to my farm. Write me at Marion, Va. The letter will be sent forward.

With love
Sherwood Anderson

81

Hotel Willmar
Willmar, Minnesota
[December, 1934]

Dear Gertrude Stein—

Your letter reached me out in the big snow country and I am not sure I will be able to catch up with you—just to see you for a moment anyway—as I hope.

I mean at Minneapolis—

If not that I'll try Richmond—in January.

Good going.
Sherwood Anderson

50. Carl Van Vechten (1880–1964), the American novelist who had met Gertrude Stein in Paris before World War I and who remained her friend and became her literary executor until 1958.

82

Ripshin Farm
Trout Dale, Va.
[December, 1934]

Dear Gertrude Stein & Alice—

We got home yesterday and I sent one of the rugs you liked, thinking it would be nice in your Paris house.

Also I wrote to Lloyd Lewis—the General Sherman man, telling him to come and see you when you got to Chicago.[51]

On the way home we stopped at Columbus but did not read the newspaper and did not find out, until too late, that you were there and we might have heard you—

We tried, with no success, to get into touch—

The book, containing the essay on Gertrude, and other Americans—is being published by Centaur Press—Philadelphia. I haven't got copies yet. It is called *No Swank.*[52]

Are plans for going South, perhaps into Mexico, in early January—are not definite yet. When they are I will write you.

Lots of love to you both
Sherwood

83

The Commodore Perry
Toledo, Ohio
[December 21, 1934]

My dear Sherwood,

What a shame, that we should have been in Columbus the same day and did not meet, and there were so many ways that

---

51. Lloyd Lewis (1891–1949), Chicago journalist, author of *Sherman, Fighting Prophet* (New York: Harcourt, Brace, 1932). Lewis did not live to complete a multivolume biography of Ulysses S. Grant.

52. "Gertrude Stein," Item 75 above, in *No Swank* (Philadelphia: Centaur Press, 1934), pp. 81–85.

we could should and would have met and they all went the wrong way and I am sorrier than I can say because we did have such a good time together in Stillwater and more of the same would have been just right but anyway it will happen later. I liked your article a lot, I like the fact that you can and do see them where they are, and where you are, my dear, there is only you doing that, but we will meet again and love to them all and a good Christmas to you whether it is warm or cold a good Christmas all the same and all really includes you all, and John and Marion too, and all of you. Lots of love always

Gtde.

84

Ripshin Farm
Trout Dale, Va.
[December, 1934]

Dear Gertrude Stein

I forgot to tell you when I wrote that I have already written a note to Lloyd Lewis, who wrote the grand book on General Sherman, to look you up while you are in Chicago.

Lewis can be reached by phone—editorial dept., Chicago *Daily News.*

Sherwood

85

[?Chicago, December 26, 1934]

My dear Sherwood,

Oh thanks and thanks again for the lovely rug, it gives us so much pleasure now and will give us so much pleasure in Paris, I can't tell you what a delight it is to us and it walked in so pleasantly day before Christmas just as something from you would come, you always come unexpectedly and naturally and that is an unending delight. Our plans are steadily shaping for our Southern trip and it will be wonderful being together in Va or in New Orleans or somewhere, it's a lovely American continent and it is very lovely that we should be wandering around in it, just as we are and bumping up against each other and not just as we are. I like it a lot, I don't think one could like anything better that there may be more much more of the same is our wish for us for the New Year, and best to them all wife sister-in law and brother-in-law and love to yourself and so many thanks,

Always
Gtde.

86

The New Hotel Monteleone
New Orleans
[January, 1935]

Dear Gertrude Stein—

I had a turn of bad luck just as I was leaving home—lost my address book—so have to send this via Random House.

We left Marion, Va. about a week ago—by car—via Knoxville, Tenn.—Jackson, Miss.—Natchez and to New Orleans. I think we will go on down to Brownsville, Texas, on the gulf, and also on the border of Mexico.

If you come this way write me at Brownsville, Texas—General Delivery.

It would be great fun to see you both down here.

Lots of love,
Sherwood A[nderson]

87

Hotel Kimball
Springfield, Massachusetts.
[January, 1935]

My dear Sherwood,

Here we are as much North as you are South but we are
coming along South very soon now, we are to be in New Orleans, February 18 we go by way [of] the Carolinas and Alabama, after Virginia then we go to Chicago and then we get to
Texas around the 18 of March, I do hope that we have the luck
we did have and come together again, there is nothing else I
would like as much, we are having a fine time, lots of love to
you both

Gtde.

88

[New Orleans]
Saturday [February, 1935]

Dear Gertrude Stein. . .

I went yesterday to get the seed of the Chinese cabbage,
which I enclose. The man at the seed store told me that the
package should produce 500 plants.

I notice that by the directions on the back it suggests plant-
ing in hot beds but I did not do this. You see I have a deep
rich soil. I just planted the seed in the rows and the result
was splendid.

It was grand fun seeing you both here and every minute of
it is treasured. E[leanor] finishes her tests today and will go to
New York in a few days but I will stay on here, for perhaps a
month. I may go out to the gulf, to a place where I can be out

of doors after working, but will be right here, at address on envelope, at any rate until after Mardi Gras.

Lots of love to you both.

Sherwood

Will be at Buena Vista Hotel, Lee Circle, New Orleans. . . perhaps for some weeks.

89

The Midway Drexel Apartment Hotel
Chicago
[February 26, 1935]

My dear Sherwood,

Thanks for the seeds but Alice is going to tell you all about that but thanks awfully for everything, my hook rug and the corn and cabbage seeds will this summer be all that we have of America, and we are both dropping tears about it, after we left you we flew and flew and here we are and are to be here for two weeks and here it is most wonderfully snowing, I don't know which we like best I guess we like it all best and really I can only see a possible future of wandering around this land and meeting up with you and Eleanor and wandering around this land and meeting up with you and Eleanor, that is the way the only way we see our future, it is a lovely land so white and blue and lovely, the Mississippi was fine at St Louis, and it was fine from the air and it was finest at New Orleans, and the wonderful squares of land in Mississippi well anyway we are glad that Eleanor's tests passed alright and we must meet in Texas and so much love and lots of love

Gtde

90

Dear Gertrude and Alice. . .

It is very hot in New Orleans this morning. I just came back here and got your letter. E[leanor] went to New York and I went off to the country. I went to an island, in the gulf, one of the places, among thousands, I have wanted you two to see. I think it is because I have felt in you both, with real sincerity, love of seeing, hearing, smelling about America. It's too dead in most people. It does good to feel it in you.

The place to which I went is an island, inhabited since before the revolution, French, Spanish, Indians and Negroes, all gradually intermarried. They fish. There is no agriculture.

A city man owned land on the island and built a ramshackle hotel, putting his mistress in charge, wanted to get rid of her I guess. It was a crazy place, the landlady always half drunk, crazy plumbing, mostly none. A beautiful beach.

Nights spent on the beach fishing, alone. I hauled out big fish. Don't tell Hemingway. I dare say he would have loved seeing them suffer. It was all moonlight nights and big porpoises swam around me as I walked out into the surf, in my hip boots, to cast my line. It gets you kinda crazy the beauty of things sometimes.

Plans hang. I expect E[leanor] back here about the 28th. Then she has to go to a lot of places, West Palm Beach, Macon, Ga., Atlanta, etc., etc. and I'll drive her. We should be back in Virginia by this time next month and then may go East. . . where I hope we will get one more look at you two.

Love
Sherwood

91

The Midway Drexel Apartment Hotel
Chicago
[March, 1935]

My dear Sherwood,

We could not resist any longer, we hired ourselves a drive yourself car and we have driven it all day, to-night we got lost in the wilds of Chicago parks and we were two hours late for dinner but it was wildly xciting, no there is no doubt about it we will permanently take to the road and will we see you in Texas we get there on the seventeenth and stay about a week, do let us hear your plans, it was most awfully nice seeing you and we do so awfully want more of the same

Love to you both
Gtde.

The seed is on its way to be planted.

92

The Midway Drexel Apartment Hotel
Chicago
[March, 1935]

My dear Sherwood,

Here we are starting off to Texas I do hope we will see you there somewhere, did you get my last two letters, I saw a lot of Lewis here and liked him so much, love to you both, and lots of it, address 18 to 20 / care of Miss Hockaday, Hockaday School, Dallas Texas after that Algonquin Hotel.

Gtde.

93

Hotel Mark Hopkins
San Francisco
[April, 1935]

My dear Sherwood,

I have just got hold of your book *Puzzled America*[53] and I like it a lot, I have read it and am still reading it, I think you have got a lot down all over but the South is wonderful and the introduction some of your very best writing, I think your writing is progressively getting more power and more simplicity, I do not think anybody has written a more direct description of anything since Young's travels on the continent at the end of the eighteenth century,[54] I am terribly pleased about it all, here we are and now we fly back to Chicago and New York and sail for Bilignin the 4 of May, I do hope that we will be seeing you in New York before we go, our address is Algonquin Hotel 44 Street, I drove myself up from Los Angeles to here, I liked the San Joaquin and the Josemite valleys but am not so awfully keen on the rest of California, but Alice loves it and so we like it, any way lots of love to you both and the rag carpet will be a delightful feeling of you all every minute over there, but we do want to come back and drive and drive, I adore the fact that you can go up any hill without changing speeds the highways are wonderful, I am sending *Puzzled America* to Bernard Faÿ I know he will like it a lot

Always
Gtde.

53. *Puzzled America* (New York: Charles Scribner's Sons, 1935) is Anderson's collected essays on the United States in the Depression years.
54. Arthur Young (1741–1820), British defender of the French Revolution, toured France in 1787 and published *Travels in France* in 1792.

94

Hotel Algonquin
New York
[April, 1935]

My dear Eleanor

Yes we do want terribly to see you, by the way tell Sherwood that I am doing a tiny review of *Puzzled America* for the Chicago *Tribune* because I did like the book immensely, but we cannot make an evening and any way quite frankly we would as our time is so short want you and Sherwood just to lunch here with us, could you do that on the 2 of May, will you let us know right away if that suits lots of love we had a wonderful time in San Francisco, ending up with a modern/old key of the city presented by the mayor

Always
Gtde.

The second of Gertrude Stein's two reviews of Sherwood Anderson's books appeared in the Chicago Daily Tribune, 4 May 1935, p. 14.

95 GERTRUDE STEIN REVIEWS NEW ANDERSON BOOK PRAISES *Puzzled America* IN HER OWN WAY.

(This is appropriately Gertrude Stein's valedictory to her native America after the most triumphal personal tour of conquest any author has made of the United States in our day. She came on Oct. 24; she leaves New York to return to France today. She puzzled America but America didn't puzzle her.)

Puzzled America, is a way of being puzzled but is Sherwood Anderson puzzled and is he American. Yes he undoubtedly is America and American and it is puzzled his America but he is not puzzled he America because really and truly he cannot be puzzled, he and America can really and truly not be puzzled and that is what makes this book of his *Puzzled America* such an extraordinarily good book. It is a puzzled America seen by a puzzled American and it ends up by its not being possible to really puzzle America or as Sherwood Anderson is an American. In his introduction he explains all that without telling you makes you realise that a puzzled American is not a puzzled person that a puzzled America is not a puzzled land, and he makes all that come out so clearly and so truly that it makes any one glad that he Sherwood is an American and that America is that land.

I think this book is an awfully good book it is one of the very best things that Sherwood has done and that means that is one of the best books that an American has done.

It does not remind but it makes me remember that some eighteenth century Englishman and he was a farmer and he went over countries and saw them as they were, other people were puzzled then but this man saw the lands as they were. And Sherwood Anderson does really and in that way he is a farmer he sees the land as it is, and so although and really and very truly it may be entitled *Puzzled America* it is not a puzzle to him nor to the land which he covers as he knows it is there not as a puzzle but as what it is the land.

And so please every one read *Puzzled America* and see how being puzzled is being not puzzled even while every one that is any one knows that that is what is puzzling them.

I wish I could tell just how unpuzzling a puzzling thing is but and that is really what Sherwood Anderson has done and so it really has been done.

I once said of Sherwood Anderson that he was in the great American tradition that he knew what America as Mark Twain has known what it is I always have known this that Sherwood was this and now anybody can know this by the way he knows what it is when America is a puzzled America and how unpuzzled he is which is what America is. Listen to this book and you will see what I mean.

96

Dear Gertrude

It seems we won't be able to get to New York before you and Alice sail—but that doesn't make me feel as sore as the fact that you are leaving.

And you didn't see our mountain country out here. It [is] so very very beautiful now.

Gee I love you both. Do come again very soon and next time let's play a lot.

And look and look and look.

Eleanor and I both mourn—

> With all our love
> Sherwood

The book just came. I am eager to get into it.[55] You're a dear—as at last all America knows.

97

Bilignin
Par Belley
Ain
[June 10, 1935]

My dearest Sherwood,

Here we are farming, we have just planted and replanted the celery cabbage and in doing so love you more than ever, it is nice being here but golly it was nice being in America and I can't really think that we won't be at it pretty soon again, it was beautiful that American country, it was it is there is nothing to be said about it but that that it was and it is beautiful, did you see the little review I did of *Puzzled America* in the Chicago

55. On March 14, 1935, Gertrude Stein published *Lectures in America* (New York: Random House).

Tribune and did you like it, and the carpet is here with us the hook rug carpet of Virginia and it's a beauty, Alice and I are most awfully happy about it, I do wish you were both over here with us although I think on the whole what I do wish is that we were all over there with you, otherwise everything is calm I have begun to work, not very much yet but still some and how goes yours well anyway we did have a good time when we were together and all things considered we were together quite a bit and so love and lots of love to you always

Gtde.

98

27 Rue de Fleurus
[December, 1935]

My dear Sherwood,

Have not heard from you for a long time how goes it and what are you doing, we are settled down to a tranquil winter in Paris at least we hope it is going to be tranquil, they now have put off revolutions until next May, it is too cold a winter to demonstrate, we are homesick though for the land over there, this summer I did the Geographical history of America or the relation of human nature to the human mind,[56] and yesterday an American described thumbing on the roads and how near it made all those cold and warm roads perhaps we will be doing them again together, we did have a good time together in Minnesota and Louisiana, lovely woods and lovely days, well anyway lots and lots of love to you both and Merry Christmas and happy new year and best to the in-laws and best to you and oh dear I wish we were all together again, best wishes always

Gtde.

56. *The Geographical History of America or The Relation of Human Nature To The Human Mind*, introduction by Thornton Wilder (New York: Random House, 1936).

99

Dear Gertrude.

How are you and what are you up to? Lately I have been thinking of you a great deal and wondering where you are and what you are doing. We are in the country, on the Virginia farm, in the hills, and John is here. He had a job, with government, in one of the painting projects, last winter, but gave it up in the fall to devote the winter and summer to painting. It seems to me that he has been coming on pretty fast this year. Now he is making an application for a Guggenheim and I am wondering how you would feel about his using your name, as one of his references.

Eleanor and I came here in late May and, except for three weeks, spent in Colorado, where I went, to the University, to try to do a little teaching, have been here all summer. I think we will stay here until October 1st and then go, for a time, to New York. We are thinking of going to Mexico City this winter. I am publishing, this fall, a book of plays, one long and three short, and this summer have been playing with a book I call "How Green the Grass." [57] It has been a sort of play time.

As for John, I think, Gertrude, that he has a chance to become a real painter. He has never cared about anything else and it seems to me that he has both mind and feeling. Just how impartial my judgment can be I of course don't know.

As John must put in his application early in October do write me telling me whether or not it would be too presumptuous to use your name.

And lots of love to both you and Alice from all of us.

Sherwood

57. *Plays, Winesburg and Others* (New York: Charles Scribner's Sons, 1937); "How Green the Grass" remains an unfinished manuscript.

I do wish we could sometime have you and Alice here, in this
beautiful mountain country.

100

Bilignin
Par Belley
Ain
[September, 1937]

My dear Sherwood,

I would be more than delighted to god-mother John, you
know how much I liked him when he was here and I would not
be a bit surprised if he developed xceedingly well, I had dis-
tinctly the impression that there was a lot to him only the
Guggenheim people have never given the prize to any one I
backed, to be sure they have been mostly writers and they may
think my taste in painters better than that in writers no I did
back a painter Ferren and they did not give it to him but if in
view of the fact that they never have listened to me John wants
me I am only too glad to back him, we have been having a lively
summer and in November comes out *Everybody's Autobiography* the volume following *A. B. Toklas*, and I tell about how
happily we met together over there, we love you all a lot and it
would be lovely to meet again, I hope John gets it

Gtde.

101

Ripshin Farm
Troutdale, Va.
Sept. 29 [1937]

Dear Gertrude

Many thanks for your word about John's application. It is
a shot in the dark.

Not that anything is very dark. We have had a grand summer, with everything growing wonderfully, plenty of summer rains, sun, fruit and people. It is at an end now. Eleanor leaves, today, for New York but I'm staying on here. Have got to re-roof the house.

I don't know where we will go this winter but I am thinking of a month in Chicago.

And what good news that your book is on the way. It will be read eagerly. The impression of you, in America, goes on—a powerful rich thing.

> We love you,
> Sherwood A[nderson]

John is grateful to you. He will stay on, at the farm here, painting, at least until well into the winter. He has an old Ford and makes of the front seat pushed forward an easel. He drifts about in it.

Love to Alice.

Gertrude Stein wrote at length of Sherwood Anderson in the second volume of her personal memoirs, Everybody's Autobiography (New York: Random House, 1938), pp. 222–23, 256, 257, 270, 271–72.

102 FROM *Everybody's Autobiography*

When we were in St. Paul we went to Minneapolis and there I met another doctor whom I had known in the Medical School she and her husband both of them, he Ulrich had been known in those days of the Medical School as the friend of women, well anyway it was not very exciting meeting them again. And then some one told us that Sherwood Anderson was somewhere around. Ah if he was we would see him certainly we would would some one find him and some one did.

He had a sister-in-law who was married to a doctor in Fall River, Minnesota and Sherwood was traveling around to write what he thought everybody felt about farming that is the farmers. And so we were to meet at his brother-in-law's. It was winter it certainly was winter and the brother-in-law called for us to drive us out and he put a shovel in and we said what is that for and he said we would see what it was for and we did. They did not shovel us out but they shoveled somebody else out. We had a very pleasant time together. A very good Virginia dinner and a very pleasant evening altogether. They had a rug there made by an old woman in Virginia we liked so much and Sherwood said he would send us one and he did I think it was the same one and we have it in Bilignin and everybody especially French people admire it every time they see it, the pale colors are so American and the river and the house and the simple harmony of it and the taste in it, they all are astonished that they never have seen anything like that before done in America. Lord Berners who has written the music for the ballet pantomime which is to be given in March in London is also going to do the decors and he made a drawing of this carpet and is going to use it as the back drop of the stage, the name of the play is They Must Be Wedded To Their Wife but as the title is too long for advertising we call it A Wedding Bouquet. . . .

So we went away from Birmingham by airplane to New Orleans and we went over the water this time not land water but sea water and came to the large hotel in New Orleans, it seemed very political I do not suppose it was but so it seemed. Sherwood Anderson was in New Orleans and that was a pleasure and he brought us to the hotel twenty-five oranges for twenty-five cents and they were very sweet oranges and we ate them all together and it was a pleasure.

It was a pleasure it was warm like summer and Sherwood was there and he had his car and we went about together and we ate in restaurants together and we met the man who wrote

Green Pastures, in New York the one who had put it on the stage came and talked to us one day at the restaurant at the Algonquin and we went about with Miss Henderson we had known her in Paris she and her family had always been in New Orleans and she took us to see her friends in the old houses where all their portraits had been painted by the same painters as the contemporary French had been. . . we liked being in New Orleans, after all we had lived for thirty years in France and after all Alice Toklas says not but still there it is after all. . . .

We liked all we heard about Louisiana and we wanted to come back and go all around everywhere there and it was a little late for the azaleas and camelias but we saw some and we saw the little hill they built in the park to prove they had one so that New Orleans children would know a hill when they saw one and Sherwood was indignant when I complained of the Mississippi River and that I had seen it where it was not a very broad one and he took us all along it and said it is an enormous one and I said well and he said well can't you see that it is a mile deep as well as a mile wide and I said that Mark Twain's Life on The Mississippi had made it so real to me and the Saint Nicholas when I was a little girl and there was a story of a flood and I had liked that and now well there was something the matter I could not quite get used to it not looking quite as enormous as I had always seen it when I read about it and he said come again and see it and sometimes it is like that if you come again and see it you will be astonished that you did not know how wide and deep it was and looked and anyway we liked being in New Orleans. . . .

We saw a good deal of Lloyd Lewis those two weeks in Chicago and it was America that he really saw whatever else he saw. . . .

I am always wanting to collaborate with some one I wanted to collaborate with Sherwood Anderson in a history of Grant I wanted to collaborate with Louis Bromfield in a detective story and now I want to collaborate with Lloyd Lewis in a history of Grant. They are all very polite and enthusiastic about it but the collaboration does never take place. I suppose I like the word collaboration and I have a kind of imagination of how it could take place. Well anyway. . . .

And so Chicago was almost over and we were going further this time it was Texas we had never been there naturally not but now we were. Sherwood had told us a good deal about it that pleased us. There was the valley his description of that was delicious. He said the valley of the Rio Grande spoken of by all Texans as the valley is perfectly flat miles of flat land just of the same flatness on either side and yet just at one moment begins the valley, only a Texan has the feeling he knows when it is just ordinary flat land and when it is a valley, it is not like the separation between the states because that is ruled lines on a map no this was more delicate you just felt that and any Texan could feel that but not any other one. We liked it and alas we never saw it we never had a chance to get to the valley we ate the fruit it made there is so much way-side fruit in America, so much way-side so much way-side and we liked all that way-side, but we did not see the valley. And then Sherwood told about how the Middle Western farmers came down for a little winter fishing in the South of Texas and how they called each other by their states, Sherwood was Virginia and he told how they talked and what they said and we wanted to have a Ford car and wander all over, we will wander all over.

103

[Marion, December, 1937]

Gertrude and Alice
Dear friends

You must excuse work paper. We are back in the hill country for the holiday season, not at the farm but in the town.

There has been heavy snow a part of the time with a strong wind blowing and now all the hills are white. I am sorry you did not get to the farm. It is up 3000 feet but there is a good road. I went up in the worst of the storm, half for the joy of seeing it and being in it in the storm.

We left the farm in October and went to Mary Emmett's farm, up the Hudson above N. Y. E[leanor] commuted back and forth and I stayed there to work. Then into the city for about two weeks and back here. We are going to leave here about Jan. 15th and go to Arizona, down into the desert country on the Mexican border.

About work . . . I am having a lot of fun with a novel, wrote it once, on the farm this summer, but am completely rewriting it. I hope to get to the end of that before long.

And then I have a real project. I am going to try to write a history of the Civil War. Have been aching to get at the job since I was a boy and now am going to tackle it. Half my traveling and reading all my life has been for this. It is in some way in my blood. I hardly know how we will manage to finance it but I'm going to start anyway.

I do hope you will come back when you can play more. Lots of love from us both.

Sherwood

104

5 Rue Christine
[January, 1938]

My dear Sherwood,

Happy New Year to you and yours, and did they give it to John, they never do to any one they should and they should to him, I do hope he was the xception to prove the rule, you see by the above that we are moving, I guess 27 got so historical it just could not hold us any longer and so the landlord wanted to put his son in and we might have made a fuss but we were kind of pleased and now we are very pleased, I hope you will come to the new place, it would please us as much as when you came to the old place and you know what a lot that was, and did they send you my new book I told them to and I hope you liked it it would please me if you did, and lots of love now and always

Gtde.

105

Chicago
Jan. 24th [19]38

Dear Gertrude. . .

Your letter came to me here. I am wandering again. Why did you not come back with no other purpose than to wander with me? From here we . . . Eleanor and I . . . are heading south. We are driving. I am a bit uncertain where we will land but we are going to move toward Mexico. John was asked to send some canvasses to New York, I dare say to be looked at by some painters appointed by the Guggenheim. Both John and myself are mighty grateful to you for your word to help. I believe no one will know before there is a public announcement, sometime, I think, in the spring.

John has just got himself married, to a school teacher. She seems o.k. They are going to move down into Virginia, she to teach school there. As you know Bob runs some weekly newspapers and John has made himself a competent runner of the line-o-type machine. He will work certain hours and hopes, if the Guggenheim doesn't come off, to have some time for painting. We are all well. I keep milking the cow but, just at present, I am waiting for the cream to rise.

Lots of love to you and to Alice. As for your new book, it arrived at the house before Christmas. It became a kind of

Bible in the house. We kept reading it aloud. Mother declared it is the wisest of all books.

Sherwood A[nderson]

106

5 Rue Christine.
[February, 1938]

My dear Sherwood,

The only thing we could possibly like better than wandering with you is this delightful new home we have just made ourselves, these things do happen, perhaps you will come and wander here, why not, not such bad wandering after all, and I do hope John gets it but they are such awfully obstinate asses those people, I can't think of John as married, he was so completely the young adolescent when we knew him, and then he will be a father, nothing to be done about that, well keep milking the cow as long as it does not get foot and mouth disease as alas all the cows at Bilignin have there is a pleasure, milk is better than cream anyway and a cow is the best of all, dear Sherwood love and lots of it to you all

Always
Gtde

107

The Miller Hotel
Brownsville, Texas
April 1, 193[8]

Dear Gertrude

I will have to send this to the old address because I cannot make out the new one. Your writing, like my own, has a certain mystic quality. It seems strange to think of you two in any place other than the beautiful rooms in the Rue de Fleurus.

Eleanor and I have been down into old Mexico. We went clear down, past Mexico City, to the southwest, to the Pacific, in the car, turning back at a place called Acapulco, where we had marvelous bathing on wide beautiful beaches. Most of the trip was over mountains, sometimes ten thousand feet up. It was certainly a new America to us, in the people, for the most part Indians, something very bitter and cruel, something very rhythmic and laughing.

We are on our way home now and got your letter here.

As for John, I haven't heard.[58] He has got a little house in the country and is painting. God knows what will best bring out the poet in such a young painter. It may be that marriage will work for him.

I wish we could come to see you in your new place. It was a satisfaction always to think of you in the place we knew.

Lots of love to you both. I hope you are working away.

Sherwood

108
[Paris, December, 1938]

My dear Sherwood,

Merry Christmas and happy New Year to you and to all of you, you are there and we are here and I wish it might be that we were together, we did have an awfully good time together, I do so often think about those oranges in New Orleans and the ham in the snow, and beside you do not know how much everybody loves the Virginia rug, Berners is using it as the background for the pantomime he is doing with me,[59] it is a

58. John Anderson did not receive a Guggenheim award.
59. Lord Gerald Berners (1883–1950) did not finally write the music for Stein's "Doctor Faustus Lights the Lights," written in 1938.

wonderful bit of America in France, so much happens, any-where just now, but what happens best is when we are to-gether, we have no plans, not at present anyway, and you, do give yourself all our love and best to all yours and America always

Gtde.

109

Trout Dale
Virginia
Sept. 21 [19]40

Dear Gertrude. . .

Max Perkins of Scribner's came down to see me and brought me your new book, which I find very delightful.[60]

I have been very anxious to hear from you. Are you well? Are you in Paris? Is there any chance you may soon be coming to America?

Do let me hear from you.

All my love
Sherwood Anderson

110

The Royalton
New York
Monday Nov. 4 [1940]

Dear Gertrude. . .

For a long time I kept thinking of you and Alice as in Paris and then someone told me that you were in America. They

60. Maxwell Perkins (1884–1947), Charles Scribner's Sons' famous editor, who was working to publish Anderson's final memoirs; Gertrude Stein's "new book" was *Paris France* (New York: Charles Scribner's Sons, 1940).

said that you were in Topeka, Kansas. They seemed to think you were hiding there, you and Alice.

And then I heard that you were both in New York, that you had come in secretly, disguised as someone else. No one seemed to be able to tell me why you should do that.

Then Max Perkins of Scribner's came down into the country to see me. He said that he had your new book and that I could write to you. He went home and sent me the book which I loved. However he did not think to tell me that you were not in Paris so, although I had written there and had got no answer, I wrote again.

I kept being afraid that something dreadful might have happened.

Then I saw the piece you wrote for *Harper's* magazine[61] and understood that you must be in a place surprisingly like the place in which we live most of the year, the same sort of mountain country, women in the fields, the cows, plenty of firewood, etc.

Then we came to New York to this hotel and yesterday I went to the Stettheimers' and saw Virgil Thomson who gave me this address and I was made happy to think that you were all right.

Love to you both
Sherwood Anderson

111

Bilignin par Belley (Ain)
[December, 1940]

My dearest Sherwood,

I can't tell you how happy and pleased and all we were at our getting your letter. As it happened we happened to have

61. Probably Stein's "The World is Round," *Harper's Bazaar*, June 1939, pp. 46–47, 92, 94, 95, 96.

been talking a lot about you lately, and wondering the way one does these days where you were and what you were doing as one does wonder these days although actually mostly everybody is staying where they are rather more than less than usual. It happened that your envelope having just come was lying on the table and Balthus, perhaps one of the most interesting of the young painters and who is also passing winters and summers not far from us had bycycled over, and he said, what a nice handwriting. It is Sherwood Anderson I said, well said Balthus meditatively he is the one I like and admire most of all the American writers, he is the only one that has the real America in him, I have read them all and perhaps I like *Many Marriages* best, and so we talked about you a long time and he hopes someday to meet you, you probably have heard of him. Yes this country is just like that and somehow one gets so every day into the country that what else can you do. Cities seem so very far away and not interesting, so here we are, helas the letters written to Paris have never come out, but do write again, you don't know what a pleasure it is to see first the envelope and then the letter, Alice smokes ham in your manner, cooking it in milk, and we talk about the good days we had together and love to you both and lots of it

Gtde.

On February 28, 1941, Sherwood and Eleanor Anderson sailed from New York for a good-will tour of South America. Anderson died of peritonitis in the Panama Canal Zone on March 8, 1941. The following letter, the last from Anderson to Gertrude Stein, was remailed on November 2, 1941, by Eleanor Anderson, who described it as "a letter which Sherwood wrote you before we left for South America—I hope that you will get it this time. He spoke of you with affection often."

112

The Hotel Royalton
New York, New York
January 26, 1941

Dear Gertrude:

I was very much delighted to get your letter and hear the news of your house, of Alice and of how you are spending your days.

As you have perhaps heard, there is a great deal of stir over here now. Fortunately, both of my sons are married and have children so will probably not be induced into the army. I had a truck we use in our Virginia farm and I loaned it to John this fall. He packed a few household goods in the truck and went off south to a little fishing village down on the Gulf of Mexico called Apalachicola, Florida. He is spending the winter down there among the fishermen and writes that he is painting. The other son, whom I believe you did not meet, is running the newspapers down in our town in Virginia.

Eleanor and I are now planning to go off to South America late in February. We have a passage engaged on a boat and plan to take a long sea voyage and land far down somewhere on the west cost, probably in Chile. We may stay down there several months.

I dare say you have heard of Hemingway's huge success with his new book and of the sudden death of Scott Fitzgerald.[62] I guess poor Scott has had a rather rough time. His wife went insane and he himself rather went to pieces, overdrinking badly. He had for some time been making his living as a movie writer out in Los Angeles.

62. Ernest Hemingway, *For Whom the Bell Tolls* (New York: Charles Scribner's Sons, 1940); F. Scott Fitzgerald died on December 21, 1940.

I keep hoping that you may be heading back to this country, one of these days, and perhaps living with us over here.

In the meantime, all our love to you and Alice.

Sherwood Anderson

The last published tribute to Sherwood Anderson from Gertrude Stein appeared in the Anderson memorial issue of the magazine Story 19 (September–October 1941): 63. Miss Stein apparently did not write of Anderson again before her own death after an operation for cancer in France on July 27, 1946.

113 SHERWOOD'S SWEETNESS

Yes undoubtedly, Sherwood Anderson had a sweetness, and sweetness is rare. Once or twice somebody is sweet, but everything in Sherwood was made of this sweetness. Here in war-time France they have made a new sugar, grape sugar, and it is as sweet as sugar and it has all through it the tang of a grape. That was Sherwood's sweetness, it was like that.

I had a letter from him, just before he died, and when I read the letter, well it just said how do you do and how are you and glad to have heard from you, but all of it had this quality of sugar made out of grapes, it just naturally was this grape sugar substance in everything Sherwood did or was. And he was everything and he did everything.

Funny I always connect Sherwood with sweet fruits. I remember in New Orleans when he came into the room he had a bag of oranges, twenty-five for twenty-five cents, and he and we ate all the twenty-five oranges; they were orange sweet, the kind that are twenty-five oranges for twenty-five cents way are orange sweet.

Dear Sherwood, as long as grape sugar is grape sugar and it always is, and oranges twenty-five for twenty-five cents are oranges, so long will Sherwood be Sherwood. And as grape sugar will always be, and oranges will always be, so will he.

One cannot cry when grape sugar is like that or twenty-five oranges for twenty-five cents are like that, and one cannot die when they are like that, so one does not cry for Sherwood nor does Sherwood die.

No.

Grape sugar and oranges twenty-five for twenty-five cents, they are Sherwood.

A NOTE ON EDITING AND PUBLISHING

The idea for this book of letters and essays came to me early in 1966 when I was starting to publish a small series of Sherwood Anderson editions with The University of North Carolina Press. Over lunch with Lambert Davis, now director emeritus of the Press, I casually mentioned my interest in the Anderson-Stein friendship and the existence of both sides of the authors' correspondence. To my surprise and delight, he thought the project worth pursuing for his Press—if our first Anderson volumes were well received.

When The University of North Carolina Press published The Achievement of Sherwood Anderson in the fall of 1966 and the literary public received the book well, we began to explore with the estates of Sherwood Anderson and Gertrude Stein the possibility of my editing the authors' correspondence. I was able to expect cooperation from the Anderson Estate, but I had no idea how Miss Stein's executors would react to my proposal. Late in the winter of 1966–67, Lambert arranged to talk in New Haven with Mr. Donald Gallup, Miss Stein's literary executor, who was planning to publish an edition of Stein letters with the Yale University Press. Mr. Gallup was encouraging to my project.

When our next two Anderson books (Return to Winesburg, 1967; and Sherwood Anderson's Memoirs, 1969) had proved successful, Lambert began correspondence in December, 1969, with Mr. Gallup and Mr. Calman Levin (representing the Stein Estate) and with Mr. Ivan von Auw and Miss Patricia Powell of Harold Ober Associates (representing the Anderson Estate). Having promised not to burden me with details of his negotiations, Lambert settled what must have been complicated problems of publication rights, for, just before his retirement from The University of North Carolina Press in the summer of 1970, he wrote me of his delight in finally having a contract for our book.

The legal arrangements settled, I was ready to prepare the manuscript documents and the published essays for my volume. I spent most of the summer of 1971 at The Newberry Library in Chicago and at The Beinecke Rare Book and Manuscript Library of Yale University. The Beinecke owns Anderson's letters to Miss Stein and photocopies of her letters to Anderson. The Newberry holds Miss Stein's letters to Anderson and photocopies of his letters to Miss Stein.

Reading, transcribing, and editing manuscript material by Sherwood Anderson is by now no problem to me. Many of his letters to Miss Stein are typed, some from dictation and some by Anderson himself. I have in this text presented Anderson's letters with his format intact, but I have felt licensed to correct his spelling and to supply an occasional omitted mark of punctuation.

To edit Miss Stein's manuscript material is entirely another matter. None of her letters is typed, and her script is very hard to decipher. As I am certainly a novice at transcribing the handwriting of Gertrude Stein, I used Mr. Gallup's occasional transcriptions of her letters to correct my vague guesses. But there were times when Mr. Gallup and I disagreed over Miss Stein's intended words and at least one time when neither of us could even guess at her intentions. I have bracketed such instances in this text, along with any other conjectural material or missing information. Because with Gertrude Stein punctuation and paragraphing may be part of her message, I have dared tamper with her format only in punctuating the titles of literary works mentioned by her. As with Sherwood Anderson, Miss Stein's published work reprinted here is from the printed instead of the extant manuscript sources.

I have in footnotes identified, whenever possible or necessary, allusions by the two authors to their own or others' literary works and references to people discussed by name. The documentation and linking material I have deliberately minimized so that the correspondence and the essays themselves can demonstrate the extent and the depth of this appealing literary friendship.

A SELECTED BIBLIOGRAPHY

I. BOOKS BY SHERWOOD ANDERSON

Windy McPherson's Son. New York: John Lane Company, 1916.
Marching Men. New York: John Lane Company, 1917.
Mid-American Chants. New York: John Lane Company, 1918.
Winesburg, Ohio. New York: B. W. Huebsch, 1919.
Poor White. New York: B. W. Huebsch, 1920.
The Triumph of the Egg. New York: B. W. Huebsch, 1921.
Horses and Men. New York: B. W. Huebsch, 1923.
Many Marriages. New York: B. W. Huebsch, 1923.
A Story Teller's Story. New York: B. W. Huebsch, 1924.
Dark Laughter. New York: Boni and Liveright, 1925.
Sherwood Anderson's Notebook. New York: Boni and Liveright, 1926.
Tar: A Midwest Childhood. New York: Boni and Liveright, 1926.
A New Testament. New York: Boni and Liveright, 1927.
Hello Towns! New York: Horace Liveright, 1929.
Perhaps Women. New York: Horace Liveright, 1931.
Beyond Desire. New York: Liveright, Inc., 1932.
Death in the Woods. New York: Liveright, Inc., 1933.
No Swank. Philadelphia: Centaur Press, 1934.
Puzzled America. New York: Charles Scribner's Sons, 1935.
Kit Brandon. New York: Charles Scribner's Sons, 1936.
Plays, Winesburg and Others. New York: Charles Scribner's Sons, 1937.

Home Town. New York: Alliance Book Corporation, 1940.

Sherwood Anderson's Memoirs. New York: Harcourt, Brace and Company, 1942.

The Sherwood Anderson Reader. Edited by Paul Rosenfeld. Boston: Houghton Mifflin Company, 1947.

The Portable Sherwood Anderson. Edited by Horace Gregory. New York: Viking Press, 1949.

Letters of Sherwood Anderson. Edited by Howard Mumford Jones and Walter B. Rideout. Boston: Little, Brown and Company, 1953.

Sherwood Anderson: Short Stories. Edited by Maxwell Geismar. New York: Hill and Wang, 1962.

Return to Winesburg: Selections from Four Years of Writing for a Country Newspaper. Edited by Ray Lewis White. Chapel Hill: University of North Carolina Press, 1967.

A Story Teller's Story: A Critical Text. Edited by Ray Lewis White. Cleveland: Press of Case Western Reserve University, 1968

Sherwood Anderson's Memoirs: A Critical Edition. Edited by Ray Lewis White. Chapel Hill: University of North Carolina Press, 1969.

Tar: A Midwest Childhood, A Critical Text. Edited by Ray Lewis White. Cleveland: Press of Case Western Reserve University, 1969.

The Buck Fever Papers. Edited by W. D. Taylor. Charlottesville: University Press of Virginia, 1971.

Marching Men: A Critical Text. Edited by Ray Lewis White. Cleveland: Press of Case Western Reserve University, 1972.

II. BOOKS AND PERIODICALS ABOUT SHERWOOD ANDERSON

Asselineau, Roger, ed. *Configuration Critique de Sherwood Anderson*. Published in *La Revue des Lettres Modernes*, nos. 78–80 (1963).

Anderson, David D. *Sherwood Anderson*. New York: Holt, Rinehart and Winston, 1967.

Burbank, Rex. *Sherwood Anderson*. New York: Twayne Publishers, 1964.

Chase, Cleveland B. *Sherwood Anderson*. New York: R. M. McBride, 1927.

Fagin, Nathan Bryllion. *The Phenomenon of Sherwood An-*

derson: *A Study in American Life and Letters*. Baltimore: Rossi-Bryn, 1927.

Howe, Irving. *Sherwood Anderson*. New York: William Sloane, 1951.

Newberry Library Bulletin, 2d ser. no. 2 (December 1948). The Sherwood Anderson Memorial Number.

Newberry Library Bulletin 6, no. 8 (July 1971). The Special Sherwood Anderson Number.

Schevill, James. *Sherwood Anderson: His Life and Work*. Denver: University of Denver Press, 1951.

Shenandoah 13 (Spring 1962). The Sherwood Anderson Number.

Story 19 (September–October 1941). The Sherwood Anderson Memorial Number.

Sutton, William A. *Exit to Elsinore*. Muncie, Ind.: Ball State University, 1967.

Weber, Brom. *Sherwood Anderson*. Minneapolis: University of Minnesota Press, 1964.

White, Ray Lewis, ed. *The Achievement of Sherwood Anderson: Essays in Criticism*. Chapel Hill: University of North Carolina Press, 1966.

―――. *Checklist of Sherwood Anderson*. Columbus, Ohio: Charles E. Merrill, 1969.

―――. *Studies in Winesburg, Ohio*. Columbus, Ohio: Charles E. Merrill, 1971.

III. BOOKS BY GERTRUDE STEIN

Three Lives. New York: Grafton Press, 1909.

Tender Buttons. New York: Claire Marie, 1914.

Geography and Plays. Preface by Sherwood Anderson. Boston: Four Seas Company, 1922.

The Making of Americans Being a History of a Family's Progress. Paris: Contact Editions, 1925.

Composition as Explanation. London: Hogarth Press, 1926.

Useful Knowledge. New York: Payson & Clarke, Ltd., 1928.

Lucy Church Amiably. Paris: Plain Edition, 1931.

Before the Flowers of Friendship Faded Friendship Faded. Paris: Plain Edition, 1931.

How to Write. Paris: Plain Edition, 1931.

Operas and Plays. Paris: Plain Edition, 1932.

Matisse Picasso and Gertrude Stein. Paris: Plain Edition, 1933.
The Autobiography of Alice B. Toklas. New York: Harcourt, Brace and Company, 1933.
Four Saints in Three Acts. New York: Random House, 1934.
Portraits and Prayers. New York: Random House, 1934.
Lectures in America. New York: Random House, 1935.
Narration. Introduction by Thornton Wilder. Chicago: University of Chicago Press, 1935.
The Geographical History of America or The Relation of Human Nature to the Human Mind. Introduction by Thornton Wilder. New York: Random House, 1936.
Everybody's Autobiography. New York: Random House, 1937.
Picasso. London: B. T. Batsford, Ltd., 1938.
Paris France. London: B. T. Batsford, Ltd., 1940.
What Are Masterpieces. Los Angeles: Conference Press, 1940.
Ida A Novel. New York: Random House, 1941.
Wars I Have Seen. New York: Random House, 1945.
The Gertrude Stein First Reader & Three Plays. Dublin and London: Maurice Fridberg, 1946.
Brewsie and Willie. New York: Random House, 1946.
Selected Writings of Gertrude Stein. Edited by Carl Van Vechten. New York: Random House, 1946.
Four In America. Introduction by Thornton Wilder. New Haven: Yale University Press, 1947.
Last Operas and Plays. Edited by Carl Van Vechten. New York: Rinehart & Company, 1949.
Things as They Are. Pawley, Vt.: Banyan Press, 1950.
Two: Gertrude Stein and Her Brother and Other Early Portraits (1908–1912). Foreword by Janet Flanner. New Haven: Yale University Press, 1951.
Mrs. Reynolds and Five Earlier Novelettes (1931–1942). Foreword by Lloyd Frankenberg. New Haven: Yale University Press, 1952.
Bee Time Vine and Other Pieces (1913–1927). Preface by Virgil Thomson. New Haven: Yale University Press, 1953.
As Fine as Melanctha (1914–1930). Foreword by Natalie Clifford Barney. New Haven: Yale University Press, 1954.
Painted Lace and Other Pieces (1914–1937). Introduction by Daniel-Henry Kahnweiler. New Haven: Yale University Press, 1955.

Stanzas in Meditation and Other Poems (1929–1933). Preface by Donald Sutherland. New Haven: Yale University Press, 1956.

Alphabets and Birthdays. Introduction by Donald Gallup. New Haven: Yale University Press, 1957.

A Novel of Thank You. Introduction by Carl Van Vechten. New Haven: Yale University Press, 1958.

Writings and Lectures, 1911–1945. Edited by Patricia Meyerowitz. London: Peter Owen, 1967.

Selected Operas and Plays of Gertrude Stein. Edited by John Malcolm Brinnin. Pittsburgh: University of Pittsburgh Press, 1970.

Fernhurst, Q.E.D., and Other Early Writings. Introduction by Leon Katz. New York: Liveright, 1971.

IV. BOOKS ABOUT GERTRUDE STEIN

Bridgman, Richard. *Gertrude Stein in Pieces*. New York: Oxford University Press, 1970.

Brinnin, John Malcolm. *The Third Rose: Gertrude Stein and Her World*. Boston: Little, Brown, 1959.

Gallup, Donald, ed. *Flowers of Friendship: Letters Written to Gertrude Stein*. New York: Alfred A. Knopf, 1953.

Haas, Robert Bartlett, and Gallup, Donald Clifford. *A Catalogue of the Published and Unpublished Writings of Gertrude Stein*. New Haven: Yale University Library, 1941.

Hoffman, Frederick J. *Gertrude Stein*. Minneapolis: University of Minnesota Press, 1961.

Hoffman, Michael J. *The Development of Abstractionism in the Writings of Gertrude Stein*. Philadelphia: University of Pennsylvania Press, 1965.

Miller, Rosalind S. *Gertrude Stein: Form and Intelligibility*. New York: Exposition Press, 1949.

Reid, Benjamin Lawrence. *Art by Subtraction*. Norman: University of Oklahoma Press, 1958.

Rogers, W. G. *When This You See Remember Me: Gertrude Stein in Person*. New York: Rinehart, 1948.

Sawyer, Julian. *Gertrude Stein: A Bibliography*. New York: Arrow Editions, 1941.

Sprigge, Elizabeth. *Gertrude Stein: Her Life and Work*. New York: Harper, 1957.

Stewart, Allegra. *Gertrude Stein and the Present*. Cambridge,
   Mass.: Harvard University Press, 1967.
Sutherland, Donald. *Gertrude Stein: A Biography of Her
   Work*. New Haven: Yale University Press, 1951.
Toklas, Alice B. *The Alice B. Toklas Cook Book*. New York:
   Harper, 1954.
————. *What Is Remembered*. New York: Holt, Rinehart
   and Winston, 1963.

INDEX

A

American Mercury, 36–37
American Spectator, 80, 85
Anderson, Cornelia Lane, 4, 70
Anderson, Eleanor Copenhaver, 84, 85, 90, 91, 92, 93, 98, 100, 102, 106, 107, 109, 112, 113
Anderson, Elizabeth Prall, 23, 39, 42, 47, 51, 52, 56, 57, 61, 62, 63, 64, 66, 67
Anderson, John Sherwood, 57, 60, 62, 65, 70, 75, 89, 100, 101, 102, 106, 107, 108, 109, 113
Anderson, Karl, 14, 15
Anderson, Margaret, 5, 33n, 37
Anderson, Marion, 57, 65, 70, 75, 89
Anderson, Robert Lane, 39, 67, 70, 107, 113
Anderson, Sherwood
    WORKS: "Alfred Stieglitz," 56n; "Brother Death," 76; "Caught," 36–37; Dark Laughter, 46, 47, 50; Death in the Woods, 76; "The Egg," 12, 42; "Explain! Explain! Again Explain," 79n; "Four American Impressions," 23–25; "Gertrude Stein," 80–84, 85, 88; Horses and Men, 34, 35; "How Green the Grass," 100; "Love and War," 39; Many Marriages, 20, 22–23, 26, 34–35, 112; "A Meeting South," 56n; No Swank, 88; Plays, Winesburg and Others, 100; Poor White, 8; Puzzled America, 95, 96–97, 98–99; Sherwood Anderson's Memoirs, 37n, 110n; Sherwood Anderson's Notebook, 53, 55, 56, 57; A Story Teller's Story, 32–33, 34, 37n, 39, 40–41, 42, 46; Tar: A Midwest Childhood, 47, 48, 50, 55, 57; The Triumph of the Egg, 12; Winesburg, Ohio, 5, 7–8, 13n, 37, 76, 77; "The Work of Gertrude Stein," 9, 10, 13, 14–17, 18, 19, 73
Anderson, Tennessee Mitchell, 6, 10, 12, 18, 20, 22, 72
Atlantic Monthly, 76, 80

B

Balthus (Klossowski de Rola), 112
Barney, Natalie Clifford, 22n, 59, 74
Beach, Sylvia, 6, 7–8, 72; Shakespeare and Company, 8n
Berners, Lord Gerald, 103, 109
Boni & Liveright, 37, 47, 50
Borrow, George, 42, 82; Lavengro, 42
Bromfield, Louis, 104
Brooks, Van Wyck, 33

C

Cambridge University, 51, 56

Turgenev, Ivan, 82
Twain, Mark, 45, 73, 97, 104; *Life on the Mississippi*, 104

U

Ulrich, Mr., 102
University of Colorado, 100

V

Van Vechten, Carl, 22n, 87

W

Wells, Whitney, 40, 42

Whistler, James M., 83
Wilder, Thornton, 62, 99n
Wilson, Edmund, 21
Woolf, Leonard, 55n
Woolf, Virginia, 55n
Wright, Lois, 25, 26

Y

Young, Arthur, 95; *Travels in France*, 95n

Z

Zola, Émile, 12

Text set in Electra Linotype

Composition, printing by
Heritage Printers, Inc., Charlotte, North Carolina

Endsheets printed by
Meredith-Webb Printing Company, Inc.
Burlington, North Carolina

Binding by
Kingsport Press, Kingsport, Tennessee

Sixty-pound No. 66 Antique paper by
S. D. Warren Company, Boston, Massachusetts

Designed and published by
The University of North Carolina Press
Chapel Hill, North Carolina